W9-AUC-570

Growing Begonias

Growing Begonias

ERIC CATTERALL

CHRISTOPHER HELM
London
TIMBER PRESS
Portland, Oregon

© 1984 Eric Catterall
Reprinted in paperback in 1985, 1989
Line drawings by David Henderson
Christopher Helm (Publishers) Ltd, Imperial House,
21–25 North Street, Bromley, Kent, BR1 1SD

ISBN 0–7470–0426–9 PBK

A CIP catalogue record for this book
is available from the British Library

All rights reserved. No reproduction, copy or transmission
of this publication may be made without written permission.

No paragraph of this publication may be reproduced, copied
or transmitted save with written permission or in accordance
with the provisions of the Copyright Act 1956 (as amended),
or under the terms of any licence permitting limited copying
issued by the Copyright Licensing Agency, 7 Ridgmount Street,
London WC1E 7AE.

Any person who does any unauthorised act in relation to
this publication may be liable to criminal prosecution and
civil claims for damages.

First published in the USA in 1984 by
Timber Press,
9999 S.W. Wilshire,
Portland,
Oregon 97225,
USA

All rights reserved

ISBN 0–917304–88–8

Printed and bound in Great Britain by
Biddles Ltd, Guildford and King's Lynn

Contents

List of Figures

Acknowledgements

Over a thirty-year period of begonia cultivation, there must have been many individuals to whom one is deeply indebted for their help and guidance. For me, one such person was the late Secretary of the National Begonia Society, Mr Fred Martin. His long years of dedication to that Society and to the growing and showing of begonias was a great inspiration, both to myself and to countless others. He helped to establish the standards of cultivation by which many of today's begonias are judged.

A regrettably all too short acquaintance with the late 'Mac' Macintyre, a man dedicated to 'the other begonias', was another experience for which I am grateful. I also acknowledge my indebtedness to the National Begonia Society for granting permission to reproduce their 'Rules for Judging Begonias' and to Rochford's Houseplants for their kind co-operation in regard to Rieger begonias. I am, by default, a person who is always willing to 'put off today what could be done tomorrow' and so my thanks go to a lady called Els who, by her constant badgering, made certain that it was indeed only tomorrow and not next year.

CHAPTER 1

History and Development of Begonias

Introduction

Botanically the family Begoniaceae comprises three genera, namely Hillebrandia, Symbegonia and Begonia. Of these genera the species, varieties and cultivars of the first two are met with only infrequently while of the latter at least 3,000 named and registered cultivars are presently grown in addition to an equal number of unnamed hybrids and a few hundred species and varieties. Estimates of the precise number of known species of the genus vary quite widely and in part this lack of agreement is most probably a consequence of the errors in naming that have occurred over the years. The prevailing view at the moment is that there are upwards of 1,000 recognisable species with not more than one quarter of them in any one collection.

Classification

When attempting to classify begonias it is necessary to note two quite distinctly different approaches which have been made, the botanical and the horticultural. The first approach is that used by botanists and taxonomists and it attempts to separate the various begonias on the basis of their flower detail. Throughout the past 100 years several such attempts have been made along these lines.

Of much greater interest to the grower of begonias however, is the horticultural classification and it is in this context that much is owed to the American Begonia Society and to the Thompsons, Mildred and Edward. In this approach the major objective has been to group together species and cultivars which have very similar growth characteristics. However, even in respect of this classification there exist two slightly different approaches.

European Classification

The system largely adopted in Europe is based on the cultivated begonias being commercially exploited. This approach leads to the following types or classes:

Elatior begonias (*B*. × Hiemalis) — the best known today are the Rieger begonias.

Lorraine begonias (*B*. × Cheimantha) — commonly known as the Christmas begonias.

Semperflorens begonias — widely used as bedding plants or in massed displays in public parks.

Tuberous begonias (*B*. × tuberhybrida) — usually thought of as the large-flowered double begonias, summer flowering. This group also includes the cascades and the multifloras.

Foliage begonias — in general these are the cultivars of *B. rex*, plants of *B. masoniana*, cultivars of *B. bowerae* and a few cane-stemmed begonias.

USA Classification

The horticultural classification adopted in the USA is more definitive and undoubtedly reflects the considerable interest in all types of begonia which exists in that country. The following classification contains within it both display and show groupings, but also brings together begonias with similar cultural requirements.

Semperflorens.   This includes the species which may grow up to 3ft tall as well as the low growing schmidtiana hybrids which are compact and under 9in high. It includes those with single or double flowers and bronze, green or variegated foliage.

Rhizomatous.   A large diversified group which will include the small, medium, large and giant sized leaf types. *B. masoniana* (B. Iron Cross) might be included here or treated separately.

Rex.   Though usually rhizomatous they are grouped separately since their highly coloured leaves in reds, silver and green together with their often varied leaf forms, e.g. spiral and non-spiral, do distinguish them from the rhizomatous group.

Cane-like.   These are the straight stemmed begonias of either the Superba or Mallet type, the latter having most attractive maroon or mahogany foliage and frequently silver spotted. Many of the cane-stemmed group are also known colloquially as 'Angel Wings'.

Figure 1.1 *Begonia masoniana* 'Iron Cross'

Shrub-like. These are sub-divided into the bare-leaved and the hairy-leaved types. They frequently require staking to maintain a shrub-like habit.

Thick-stemmed. They may be bare-leaved or hairy-leaved and often flower when leafless, e.g. *B. ludwigii*.

Tuberous. This group will include but separate the tuberous species and first generation hybrids from the Hiemalis and the Cheimantha types and tuberhybrida.

Trailing or Scandent. This group includes a number of species and cultivars of either trailing or climbing habit.

This American system of classification does allow further sub-division when required for show purposes. For example, it is not unreasonable to include *B. masoniana* with other rhizomatous begonias in a common competitive class. If, however, a number of exhibits of *B. masoniana* appear it is probably better to establish a separate competitive class for them as a sub-class of the rhizomatous types.

In the past the term 'fibrous rooted' was used to differentiate those begonias which do not have a tuber. Since every begonia has fibrous roots this term should not now be used.

Exhibition Classification

For show or exhibition purposes, the classification system

3

adopted is much simpler, at least in Great Britain. Here it is the large-flowered tuberous double begonias which are dominant and it is they which are frequently the most attractive feature in many of the summer flower shows around the country. With the possible exception of a 'hanging basket' class the schedule will be sub-divided primarily on the basis of pot plant(s) and cut blooms. Pot plants will be further separated on the basis of the number called for in the class, i.e. one, three, six or nine, and the style of growth, i.e. single or multi-stemmed. Cut blooms may be sub-divided usually on the basis of numbers and colours.

Classes for the other types of begonias are often no more specific than, say, 'Three Pots of non-tuberous begonias' or 'Six Begonias of rhizomatous type' or 'Three cane-stemmed Begonias'.

The situation in Great Britain may be summarised by noting that the schedule for the annual show of the National Begonia Society consists of 31 classes of which only three are for non-tuberous begonias; the remaining 28 include one class for a hanging basket. The schedule for the annual show of the Scottish Begonia Society has a 100 per cent requirement for tuberous double begonias. The picture in the USA contrasts sharply with that described above and it is of interest to note that at the 1982 American Begonia Society 'Begoniafest' annual convention and show only two tuberous begonias were among the winners and of these one was the species *B. gracilis*.

It would be true to say that of the combined membership of the National and the Scottish Begonia Societies probably no less than 95 per cent have the cultivation of the large-flowered tuberous double begonias as their major interest and this is reflected in the content of their respective publications. Though no precise details are available in respect of the American Begonia Society it is most likely that, judging from the contents of the publication *The Begonian*, the interest in cultivating the large-flowered tuberous doubles is far less but this is more than balanced by the enormous following for the non-tuberous species and hybrids.

This book will be directed in the main towards the successful culture of the tuberous double begonias but will also include information on the characteristics and cultivation of a number of non-tuberous types, begonias which are beginning to make an impact in Great Britain but which are already very familiar in the USA.

To understand better the environmental conditions under which begonias thrive it is instructive to note the distribution of

species world-wide. Of course the intensive breeding programmes undertaken with specific types or classes may modify
the optimum growing conditions required but basically they
remain the same.

For many years the American Begonia Society's journal *The
Begonian* has carried on its front page one of the aims and
purposes of that society, namely 'To stimulate and promote
interest in Begonias and other shade loving plants'. These
words might be interpreted as meaning that begonias are able to
thrive only in very low light levels; while this might be partly
true, it is nevertheless somewhat misleading.

Unduly low light levels will surely result in spindly growth
and severe yellowing of the foliage. The very lush growth found
with many begonias needs adequate light to ensure the
necessary levels of photosynthesis.

The majority of species begonias prefer to be protected from
the effects of exposure to the hot midday sun and they also like
to be close to ample supplies of water so that adequate levels of
atmospheric humidity can be maintained. A very small number
have their origins in locations which are frequently bathed in
cloud.

It is, therefore, not surprising that by far the greater number
of begonia species have been discovered in the tropical and near
tropical areas of the world and especially on the South
American continent in Mexico, Brazil, Argentina, Peru and
Uruguay. The West Indies and South Africa have provided a
number of species and even fewer (most notably *B. rex*) have
been discovered in China, the Himalayas, Bengal and Sri Lanka.
In a general way the origins of the family Begoniaceae indicate
that they will thrive in humid, warm conditions where the light
levels are good but not in direct sunlight.

The botanical history of the genus Begonia has been well
documented elsewhere and only the essential highlights will be
recorded here. The story of discovery began in or around 1650
when Francisco Hernandez incorrectly listed a plant — originally discovered in 1570 — as Totoncaxoxo coyollin. This plant is
now correctly known as *B. gracilis*. After a slow start the rate of
discovery of new species increased rapidly during the seven-
teenth, eighteenth and nineteenth centuries. Much of the work
of discovery was undertaken by European plant hunters,
initially on behalf of botanic gardens and private patrons but

then later by some of the then better known commercial nurseries.

By the middle of the nineteenth century some 350 species had been identified and listed, though not more than about 80 were in cultivation. Some hybridisation of species had been undertaken and indeed one or two cultivars had earned limited success. At this time no single type or group of begonia had fired the imagination of the man in the street, they were still very much the province of the plant hunter and the private enthusiast.

During the past 100 years there has been a most remarkable turnaround in the popularity of the begonia, a veritable upsurge in both interest and activity in the development of new cultivars. At present it is possible to identify two very well developed areas of commercial interest both of which have their origins in the discoveries of the mid-1800s.

1. The large scale production of tuberous begonias B. × tuberhybrida — some 75 million per annum in Belgium, around 3 million in West Germany and perhaps 7 million in the USA. It was in the brief seven-year period between 1860 and 1867 that Richard Pearce, on behalf of Messrs James Veitch, sent back to England four tuberous species from the South American Andes — B. boliviensis, B. pearcei, B. veitchii and B. rosaflora the latter two having been discovered at an altitude of some 12,000 ft. During the next decade a fifth species was imported from Bolivia and a sixth, B. davisii was found also at a high altitude. Each of these species bore only single flowers no more than 2¹₂ in in diameter. In that short span of some seventeen years the parents from which the present day tuberous begonias are derived came together in one commercial nursery.

2. The very considerable worldwide popularity of B. Semperflorens Cultorum ('semps') as garden bedding subjects. In the USA alone it has been estimated that at least 100 million plants are sold each year and countless more in Europe and the Far East. This well known group of begonias had its beginnings in the third quarter of the nineteenth century with the crossing of two Brazilian species B. semperflorens and the dwarf B. schmidtiana. Extensive and intensive breeding programmes have produced a wide range of flower colours including picotees, double and semi-double flowers, green and bronze foliage, tall plants and short plants etc. Indeed such has been the improvement in plant and flower quality that many cultivars are now being grown as specimen pot plants.

Two other groups of begonias are now rapidly becoming very popular as houseplants, in one case prized for their attractive foliage and in the second case for their highly colourful and long lived flowers.

1.   The widely grown begonias of the B. Rex Cultorum group-plants with very decorative leaves in reds, greens and silver and sometimes spiral shaped. Though primarily cultivated for their foliage, very often sprays of dainty pink and white flowers add their own charm. The begonia species which contributed a great deal to this colourful group was *B. rex Putzeys* fortuitously introduced into England from India in the mid nineteenth century. Astute commercial nurserymen soon began to cross this species with other rhizomatous begonias, e.g. *B. xanthina*, *B. imperialis*, *B. cathayana* and *B. diadema*. Later still even the tuberous begonia *B. evansiana* was used in breeding programmes.

2.   Most of the tuberous species and cultivars are summer flowering. In the early 1900s a winter flowering bulbous African species *B. socotrana* was introduced into Europe. Crossed with the tuberous cultivars *B. socotrana* produced many hybrids, known as the Hiemalis group, which had a much longer flowering season. In the past two decades new and improved Hiemalis type begonias known as Rieger begonias have been developed in Germany and more recently in the USA.

B. socotrana has also been crossed with a tuberous African species *B. dregei* to provide yet another range of winter-flowering plants known as the Cheimantha group. Today there is a large and ever expanding market for the Hiemalis and Cheimantha crosses which are being used as flowering house-plants and distributed through nurseries, garden centres and supermarkets.

In Great Britain alone one houseplant nursery devotes one acre of glass to the cultivation of Rieger begonias of which hundreds of thousands are sold annually to the domestic market from March to September.

More recently in the USA there has been increasing interest shown in the raising of new crosses in, for example, the cane-stemmed begonias, and indeed quite a number of named cultivars are now available. At the present time, however, this activity cannot be compared with that in the four areas noted above.

In the past 150 years or so a great many begonia species have been used in hybridising, but there is little doubt that the most concentrated and extensive efforts have been directed towards the large-flowered tuberous doubles and to a lesser extent the *B*. Rex Cultorum and Rhizomatous groups. It is instructive to examine briefly the historical development of the large flowered double begonias, one member of the *B*. × tuberhybrida group.

Historical Development

There appears to be some argument as to whether five or seven species of begonia were involved in the original development of the tuberous hybrids. The two species at the heart of the disagreement are *B. cinnabarina* and *B. clarkei*. Whatever the truth of this argument an eighth species *B. dregei* was soon to be involved since it played an important role in the production of the white-flowered tuberous hybrids. It is interesting to recall that of the original species used some four of them have their natural habitats at elevations of about 10,000 ft in the high Andes; this probably accounts for the ability of the tuberous hybrids to cope with the somewhat temperate climate of Europe.

A number of the characteristics of the modern hybrids can be traced back directly to the original species. The modern pendula or cascade begonias are the descendants of *B. boliviensis* with its tall, slender stems. The yellow-coloured tuberhybrida all have the same common parentage in *B. pearcei* while *B. cinnabarina* and *B. veitchii* contributed their strong and erect stems to the present-day hybrids.

The very first tuberous begonia hybrid B. Sedonii was exhibited by Veitch in 1869 and was the product of crossing *B. boliviensis* with, probably, *B. cinnabarina*. By 1882 Veitch had abandoned begonia breeding though considerable activity had now developed on the continent chiefly in France and Belgium. These early hybrids still only produced single flowers, but their size had been increased to about 5 in in diameter. The first doubles appeared in 1873-5 and it is generally agreed that the earliest one offered for sale was B. Montuosa (syn. B. Lemoinei). From this point on it became a matter of careful selection and breeding to further develop and refine the tuberous begonia, to extend the colour range and to improve the flower formation and plant habit.

The French, Dutch and Belgian growers concentrated their efforts towards producing tuberous double begonias which would come true to colour and 'doubleness' from seed. Today this huge commercial horticultural enterprise can virtually guarantee 100 per cent success in regard to these two characteristics and indeed it was these features which made possible the exploitation of the tuberous double begonias as suitable subjects for massed flower displays.

In England and later in the USA the objectives were somewhat different in that much more attention was given to the development of plant vigour, symmetry of bloom, flower refinement, perfect and well-defined centres and selected named cultivars.

At various times along the way a number of individual plants with characteristics differing markedly from the majority of the seedlings were discovered. These mutants were themselves developed and hybridised to give such sub-groups as:

B. × tuberhybrida (Crispa Marginata — single fringed flowers with white and yellow ground colour and pink or red margins.

B. × tuberhybrida (Fimbriata) — double flowers with serrated or fimbriated flower petals.

B. × tuberhybrida (Marmorata) — single flowers in red and pink with white dots and splashes.

B. × tuberhybrida (Multiflora) — small, single flowers on bushy, compact plants. Ideal for bedding. Probably developed from the dwarf species *B. davisii*.

B. × tuberhybrida (Multiflora Maxima) — compact, dwarf plants which hold an abundance of small, double flowers well above the foliage. Ideal for mass display work.

B. × tuberhybrida (Bertinii) — small, single, cup-shaped flowers.

B. × tuberhybrida (Pendula) — early hybrids basd on *B. boliviensis* crosses had small, single flowers with pointed tepals. Modern hybrids obtained by successive judicious crossing with tuberous double begonias have much larger and fully double flowers.

Though one or two of these (and others) have had changing fortunes in popularity over the years a number are still widely grown and annually produced by tens of thousands on the continent. Their cultivation is basically identical to that which will be described for the large-flowered tuberous double begonias. As in so many other areas of human activity fashions in begonia development change over the years. There was a period in the early 1950s when a tuberous double begonia was not considered acceptable unless it had a clearly defined perfect rosebud centre. This can be seen in such cultivars as 'Jean Padden Smith', 'Wayne Parker', 'Ivorine' and 'Rebecca'.

Large, well-rounded petals were the order of the day. A number of the very early tuberous hybrids produced flowers which had many small petals and a somewhat less well-defined centre. They bore a resemblance to the flowers of the camellia and were indeed referred to as having camellia centres. Records indicate that one large-flowered double hybrid was named, though incorrectly, as B. Camellia. Much of the begonia breeding of the post-war period both in England and the USA was directed towards refining and perfecting the 'rosebud' flower form and it is dubious whether the description 'camellia centre' now has any realistic meaning. However, what is unaccceptable today may well be the fashion of tomorrow and during the 1960s we saw the introduction of new cultivars with serrated and wavy petals, e.g. 'Ninette', 'Elaine Tartellin' etc. Though the basic rose form is still there the heavy ruffling of the petals on some modern varieties tends to obscure it.

In the last ten years there has also been a significant increase in the number and in the quality of picotee-flowered begonias.

There is undoubtedly a belief that what is new and up to date is of necessity an improvement, but it is salutary to note that in the 1951 catalogue of Messrs Blackmore and Langdon there is a black and white photograph of a begonia of almost perfect form measuring $7–7\frac{1}{2}$ in in diameter. The 1930 catalogue describes the cultivar 'Louise Arnold' which produced blooms of 8 in diameter and of good form. One must remember, however, that only in very few instances is the professional grower simply looking for increased bloom size; that is usually the major goal for many amateur exhibitors. The true horticulturalist is constantly striving for increased plant vigour, for better foliage and flower texture, for extended colour ranges, for better plant habit and bloom quality. Certainly in these respects there has been considerable progress over the past fifty years and the search is never-ending.

CHAPTER 2

Begonias in Cultivation

As we have already noted, the genus Begonia comprises at least 1,200 species to which must be added untold thousands of hybrids and cultivars. Already a number of species have disappeared and, with the extensive land reclamation and deforestation programmes going on in the Caribbean, Southern and Central America, Africa and Asia, many more will become extinct unless a greater effort in conservation is made.

Only a small fraction of the known cultivars are being cultivated today. Of course in the past this has been due to the continuing development of a particular group, but it is also a consequence of our insatiable demand for novelty year by year. All indications are that the popularity of the genus is on the increase worldwide.

For the purpose of this limited text it becomes necessary to make some arbitrary division of the begonia types being widely cultivated today. It would be nigh on impossible to make any one selection which would receive universal agreement and the one I have chosen represents a fairly pragmatic approach to begonia cultivation. The begonias to be considered below have been divided into two groups: first, those which are grown primarily for their flower quality or quantity and, second, those which are cultivated for their varied and often spectacular foliage.

Of course, as with all subjects the overall appeal lies in the total plant but, nevertheless, with begonias it is usually either the flowers or the foliage to which the eye is immediately drawn. It is hardly surprising that a number of plants in the first category will also possess most attractive foliage thus providing a lovely setting for the flowers while the beauty of many begonias in the second category is considerably enhanced by the panicles of small, but delicately coloured, florets.

It must be stressed that this book is written more for the amateur grower of begonias than the student of botany.

The begonias considered in this group are, in the main, tuberous types together with a few which are frequently described as 'fibrous rooted'. The tuberous begonias can be further sub-divided into the tuberhybrida and the tuberous species which, while well known and extensively cultivated in the USA are, with one or two notable exceptions only infrequently encountered in Great Britain and Europe.

Greenhouse Cultivation

The tuberous species begonias undoubtedly require greenhouse cultivation; this is in part due to a lack of hardiness but also to the somewhat delicate plant form. All the tuberhybrida begonias do lend themselves to garden cultivation though the true potential of the large-flowered doubles can be realised only when given greenhouse protection. Those of us who, in an official capacity, attend many of the summer shows around the country are so familiar with the popular misconception that the large, brilliantly coloured flowers of the tuberous double begonias indicate a somewhat delicate plant. The general public is convinced that high temperatures are required for the successful culture of these exotic blooms. In reality this is certainly not the case — tuberous begonias are remarkably tolerant subjects and the more usual problem encountered, even in the temperate climate of Great Britain, is how to keep the temperatures down.

Tuberhybrida
Out of doors these begonias will flower almost continuously from mid-summer to early autumn (first frosts) and provide a spectacular display as long as they are adequately protected against wind damage. A selection of tuberhybrida follows together with, where relevant, a number of desirable cultivars.

B. × tuberhybrida (Marginata) — large (5-7 in diameter) single flowers. Usually the perianth shows a narrow pink to red margin. The base colour is normally white or red — they are the picotee versions of the early single begonias.

B. × tuberhybrida (Crispa-Marginata) — also known as the 'Fascination' begonias — this group has similar colour characteristics to that above, but the perianth has fringed or frilled edges.

B. × tuberhybrida (Marmorata) — double flowers of about 5 in diameter — available in shades of carmine red splashed with white. The earlier colour range of orange, pink and scarlet seems to have become extinct.

B. × tuberhybrida (Crispa) — large single flowers, self-coloured in white, salmon, pink, red, yellow and orange with a heavily fringed or frilled perianth.

B. × tuberhybrida (Fimbriata) — double flowers of 5 in diameter with a heavily fringed perianth, often made more attractive by the contrasting yellow stamens. Colours available are red, copper, orange, pink, white and yellow.

B. × tuberhybrida (Bertinii or Bertinii Boliviensis) — a pendula type begonia with a lot of *B. boliviensis* character. The long slender stems are heavily branched giving a bushy appearance. The orange/red flowers are freely produced and are cup shaped with a pointed perianth — suitable for basket culture or even raised beds.

B. × tuberhybrida (Bertinii Compacta) — these begonias have erect flower stems and a rounded cup-shaped perianth. The flowers are single and available in the usual colours.

B. × tuberhybrida (Multiflora) — ideal begonias for bedding work, they have their origins probably in the species *B. davisii*. The plants are very compact, attaining a height of some 6-8 in. The flowers, which are profusely borne, may be single or double and around 2 in in diameter. Among a small number of select cultivars the following might be considered:

'Flamboyant' — double flowers in cherry red.

'Gent's Jewel' — double flowers in salmon.

'Helen Harms' — semi double yellow flowers.

'Mrs Richard Galle' — double flowers in orange-salmon.

B. × tuberhybrida (Multiflora Maxima) — excellent bedding begonias, very compact reaching a height of some 9 in. The small (3 in) double flowers are held well above the foliage. They are very floriferous and probably originated from crossing the large-flowered double begonias with the multiflora group. They are available in the usual colours but also in the following cultivars:

'Schweizerland' — dark red flowers and brown-green leaves.

'Masquerade' — a yellow ground, red-edged picotee.

Some of the Multiflora Maxima strains are also known as *B.* Floribunda and include such cultivars as 'Bajazzo', 'Brautjungfer', 'Mandarin' etc.

B. × tuberhybrida (Pendula) — originally developed from *B. boliviensis* the early pendulas had small cup-shaped and pointed flowers. Intensive breeding over the years using the large-flowered doubles both in England and the USA has led

13

to a strain of larger-flowered pendulas with broad petals and strong stems. Even some fragrance has been bred into one or two cultivars. Fragrance is a very rare commodity in the family Begoniaceae and in any case an individual's description is a very personal one. According to the available records some five fragrant species are known and of these *B. baumanii* and *B. micranthera fimbriata* were used in the development of the Yellow and Orange Sweeties.

Cultivars with even larger double flowers are now being made available in the 'Cascade' series. A number of cultivars worthy of consideration are:

'Apricot Cascade' — the palest orange flowers.

'Orange Cascade' — bright orange flowers in profusion.

'Pink Cascade' — very compact and free flowering.

'Picotee Cascade' — white flowers with a pale pink edge.

'Yellow Cascade' — large flowers in bright yellow.

'Scarlet Cascade' — brilliant red flowers — a magnificent sight when in full flower.

'Bridal Cascade' — white ground picotee with very fine red edge — a beautiful cultivar.

'Lou Anne' — an older cultivar — pale rose pink with large flowers.

Figure 2.1 Pendula Begonia 'Bridal Cascade'

14

'Orange Sweetie' — vivid orange with sweet scent.

'Yellow Sweetie' — pale lemon with sweet scent.

B. Lloydii — excellent for hanging baskets, grown from seed in colours of pink, red, white and yellow.

B. × tuberhybrida (large flowered doubles) — *the crème de la crème* of the tuberhybrida. Tubers grown from seed are suitable for outdoor use as bedding plants and are available in a number of named self colours, e.g. red, yellow, white, copper etc. or in bicolours or picotees. Carefully selected plants and, more especially, named cultivars should be grown as greenhouse or conservatory specimens. They may have a rose-form flower or the ruffled petal type. A number of the named cultivars are especially suited to plant culture while others are particularly valuable as cut blooms; these issues will be dealt with in Chapter 4. The following list represents a good selection of present day cultivars.

'Bernat Klein' — a brilliant white variety of good size and shape.

'Avalanche' — excellent white begonia — good depth to the flower, slightly waved petals.

'Snowbird' — pure white, deep flowers with slightly waved petals.

'Nectar' — pale blush pink — very large flowers suited for exhibition work.

'Primrose' — yellow begonias are not very common and good ones even less so. This as the name suggests is a very pale yellow with deep, slightly frilled petals.

'Carmen' — rose pink flowers. A very vigorous and floriferous cultivar.

'First Love' — deep-petalled white flowers with a clear pink margin.

'Full Moon' — very strong variety with large creamy-white flowers.

'Hawaii' — very large deep blooms in a subtle shade of orange.

'Jean Blair' — an older but excellent yellow ground picotee. First released in 1960.

'Royalty' — an early flowering crimson; as with all the cultivars of this colour the blooms are not particularly large.

'Sweet Dreams' — pale pink with slightly paler centres — extremely large blooms can be obtained with a very fine surface texture.

'Zulu' — crimson red blooms — the flower shape is traditional rose-form — very fine texture.

'Midas' — the best yellow with slightly waved petals.

'Majesty' — primrose yellow with large petalled flowers — the blooms often have a slightly 'square' look to them.

'Judy Langdon' — pale salmon pink, with huge deep flowers.

'Sugar Candy' — well named with clear pink flowers — early flowering with slightly waved petals.

'Roy Hartley' — one of the 'great begonias' — very large flowers in pink tinged with salmon.

'Falstaff' — one of the finest ever — huge deep rose-pink flowers.

'Rosalind' — rose salmon colour with broad petals.

'Red Admiral' — perhaps the best vivid red begonia — very large blooms with waved petals.

'Scarlet O'Hara' — scarlet red with large flowers held on erect stems.

'Sceptre' — large-flowered orange/scarlet with lightly frilled petals.

'Bali Hi' — rose-form flowers with slightly frilled petals — cream, or yellow ground with brilliant red picotee edge.

'Fairylight' — white ground picotee with very thin red edge and broad flat petals.

'Fred Martin' — named after the late secretary of the National Begonia Society, this is an excellent cultivar. A cream ground picotee with a fine pink edge and rose-form flowers.

'Masquerade' — a white ground picotee with a heavy red edging and crinkled petals.

'Zoe Colledge' — large, deep orange flowers.

'City of Ballarat' — named in honour of Australia's 'Begonia City', this cultivar has large, rich orange flowers produced in abundance.

'Tahiti' — very large flowers in a coral/apricot shade with ruffled petals — flowers have a tendency to produce pale centres.

'Coronet' — yellow ground picotee.

'Can Can' — very tall growing plant — rich yellow picotee with slightly serrated petals.

'Peach Melba' — very attractive flowers — almost a bicolour — pale primrose overlaid with orange.

'Honeymoon' — very broad smooth petals — rose-form flowers in pure white, edged with a fine red margin.

Tuberous Begonia Species

Very few tuberous begonia species are in general cultivation today though one or two are well worth growing. With the possible exception of *B. evansiana* they should be thought of as greenhouse subjects. Being species they do come true from seed, an advantage which they undoubtedly possess over the hybrids. Some of the species can provide welcome colour in the greenhouse over a slightly longer period than the hybrids. They can be grown as houseplants though they have a distinct tendency to shed their flower buds in a dry atmosphere. Standing the pots on a tray of wet gravel will help to prevent this. A number of worthwhile species to grow are:

B. evansiana — almost completely hardy — may be grown in the garden, producing a 2ft high shrub with pinkish-white single flowers. Bulbils form in the leaf axils and these may be used to provide new plants the following year. A pure white form *B. evansiana alba* is also available.

B. pearcei — ancestor of all the yellow and orange tuberhybrida has tiny yellow flowers held on erect stems. The medium sized leaves are velvety green and heavily veined. Only small tubers are produced.

B. cinnabarina — an untidy plant with slender stems. The orange-red flowers develop in clusters of three on erect flower stems.

B. boliviensis — an ancestor of the pendula begonias this species has long slender stems which become pendant as they develop. Very long narrow leaves and bright fuchsia-shaped flowers in a bright scarlet colour, large tubers are produced.

B. sutherlandii — a very popular houseplant with long slender stems which become pendant — very pale green leaves and small orange-red flowers. A red version is also known. Small bulbils which appear in the leaf axils may be used for propagation.

B. veitchii — an almost stemles plant from Peru which will produce vermilion red flowers up to 2 in in diameter. The dark green leaves are almost circular in shape.

B. micrantha var. venturii — a tall growing Argentinian species with large orange blooms — slightly fragrant.

All the tuberous species and the tuberhybrida share a common feature in that they require a period of dormancy each year usually during the winter months. At these times they may be removed from their pots and stored in a frost-free place.

Two types of begonia hybrid which have been making an

ever increasing impression, at least in Europe during the past 30 to 40 years are the Hiemalis and the Cheimantha groups. Both of these groups have *B. socotrana* in their breeding; this particular species which originates in Socotra, a rather hot, arid island off the African coast, is not a truly tuberous begonia but rather a bulbous one.

Hiemalis types

When crossed with the summer flowering tuberous begonias the winter flowering *B. socotrana* produces offspring which have the flowering period of the species but the flower characteristics of the tuberous parents. The resulting Hiemalis group of begonias tend to be compact plants producing many rather short basal shoots. The leaves, often in shades of a rich, dark glossy green and mahogany are about $2\frac{1}{2}$-3 in in size. The flowers which may be single, semi or fully double are produced in profusion — they usually measure some 1-$1\frac{1}{2}$ in in diameter and can be obtained in pink, white, red, salmon, yellow etc. Work during the past decade has been directed towards increasing the length of the flowering season so that the modern cultivars may now be in flower the year round with perhaps an extra flush of flower in the winter. Of this group of begonias a new improved Hiemalis type, the Rieger begonias raised in Germany, are in great demand because of their general excellence.

One or two select cultivars of the Hiemalis type are:

'Altrincham Pink' — fully double pink flowers which resemble rosebuds — Christmas flowering.
'Emily Clibran' — large double flowers in salmon pink.
'Gloire de Sceaux' — rose pink, single-flowered plant with bronze leaves.
'Nelly Visser' — rosebud-type flowers in scarlet — flowers in late autumn.

In Great Britain most of the Rieger begonias are retailed simply on the basis of bloom colour though one or two select cultivars are available, e.g.

'Fireglow' — a generic name for a variety of colours.
'Yellow Melody' — pale yellow, single flowers very freely produced.
'Aida' — single flowers in delicate pink with almost white edging; almost a picotee.

'Baluga' — bright scarlet red, single flowers; bright green foliage.

'Krefeld' — as Baluga but with bronze leaves.

The 'Aphrodite' and the 'Schwabenland' series.

Cheimantha Types

Christmas or Lorraine begonias have earned their popularity because of the wealth of bloom which they are capable of producing during the winter months (November-March) in Britain. This group is based on the crossing of *B. socotrana* with *B. dregei*, a South African semi-tuberous species which has small, rounded white flowers on short stiff stems. With this sort of parentage it is hardly surprising that some of the Cheimantha group are not really tuberous at all. For example, the most popular, and probably the best known variety, 'Gloire de Lorraine', has a fibrous root system. Though over the years a number of different cultivars have made their appearance, 'Gloire de Lorraine' is still the favourite. Two cultivars which are occasionally met with are:

'Turnford Hall' — white flowers flushed with pink.

'Mrs Leopold de Rothschild' — a larger-flowered sport of 'Gloire de Lorraine'. The Lorraine begonias produce only male flowers and are therefore sterile. Propagation is by cuttings.

Back crossing 'Gloire de Lorraine' on to *B. socotrana* produced a range of progeny with improved single flowers. One or two Cheimantha types still available are:

'Gloire de Lorraine' — pink and red single flowers — very floriferous — reddish bronze foliage.

'Lady Mac' — very lovely clear pale pink flowers.

'Ege's Favourite' — large bright reddish-pink flowers.

'Love Me' — single pink flowers very freely borne all the year round.

'Solbakken' — very stiff upright stems — has larger flowers in deep pink with yellow centres. Has more female flowers and hence will produce seed — easy to grow.

Outdoor Subjects

Of the so-called 'fibrous rooted' begonias the group most commonly met with are the 'semps' or Semperflorens Cultorum.

Semperflorens

The 'semps', or 'wax' begonias as they are also called, tend to be the Cinderellas of the begonia grower, but in fact they are among the most popular bedding plants being produced today. Over 100 million plants of Semperflorens Cultorum are sold in the USA annually with a similar number being produced in Europe.

To meet this need F1 hybrids are being raised. Whole areas are planted out with a single variety as the female or seed bearer and these are crossed with a single male or pollen parent. It is through the careful selection of the two parents that the hybrid vigour of the F1 hybrids is obtained.

In these past few years enormous strides have been made by the US and European breeders so that particular cultivars can now make exceedingly attractive pot plants or plants for hanging baskets. Many of the readily available varieties are reasonably dwarf (6-8 in) and this, together with their bushy habit, wide range of colours (except yellow) and very attractive foliage, makes them ideal subjects for bedding displays or as border plants. The modern cultivars do come true from seed so that it is possible to create mass single colour displays or to use random colour effects from mixed seed. When selecting 'semps' for a specific purpose one should bear in mind the whole plant since with these subjects the foliage tints are an integral part of the display.

The following hybrids are merely representative of the many available today.

'Snowball' — pure white single flowers with light green foliage.

'Indian Maid' — bright scarlet single flowers with deep bronze foliage — makes bushy plants.

'Dainty Maid' — very deep-pink buds which open to display white double flowers — foliage is dark green, edged with bronze.

'Flamingo' — plants grow 6in tall with white and pink flowers.

'Pink Miniature' — a very dwarf variety with rich rose-pink flowers.

'Karin' — snow-white single flowers seen at their best against the chocolate brown foliage — a shrubby plant.

'Viva' — white flowers $1\frac{1}{2}$in in diameter — green leaves on 7in tall plants.

'Scarletta' — orange-scarlet single flowers with rich green foliage.

'Saga' — bronzy-green leaves with clusters of crimson, long lasting flowers.

'Thousand Wonders' — Red, Rose and White — these cultivars of German origin have especially neat, compact habits. The foliage is bright green, with flowers borne in abundance.

'Electra' — cerise-coloured single flowers with green foliage.

'Galaxy' F1 Hybrids — masses of star-shaped single flowers — foliage deep mahogany to bronze.

'Organdy' F1 Hybrids — mixed colours set against mid-green foliage.

The above cultivars, and there are countless others, are ideal for edging and ground cover.

'Othello' — plants grow to 10in high — very dark bronze leaves — flowers in gay scarlet.

'Glamour' Series — plants 12in high — 2in diameter flowers in white, rose, red and picotee.

'Mars' — 10in high plants with green leaves and $1\frac{1}{2}$in diameter red flowers.

'Venus' — identical to Mars, but with pink flowers.

'Gladiator' — plants grow to 10in in height with a pronounced tendency to branching — red flowers with bright yellow centres.

'Frilly Pink' and 'Frilly Red' — recent introductions — the red or pink flowers are heavily frilled or ruffled — light green foliage — plants attain 10in in height.

'Rosanova' — cerise single flowers with green foliage.

'Danica Rose' and 'Danica Scarlet' — masses of rose-pink or scarlet-red single flowers with very attractive green foliage.

'Pink Ruffles' — semi-double pale pink flowers with bright green foliage.

'Salina' — dark green glossy foliage setting off a lovely display of scarlet single flowers.

'Muse Rose' — rose-pink flowers with bronze foliage.

'Pink Avalanche' — very pale pink, single flowers with light green foliage — can be good in a hanging basket.

'Loveliness' — green leaves and light pink double flowers; the flowers have golden centres and the leaves are edged with bronze.

'Ibis' — white flowers borne in profusion — green foliage.

The above cultivars are much taller reaching heights of 10-12in under ideal conditions.

These two groups of Semperflorens begonias have been developed largely as outdoor bedding plants and are extremely easy to cultivate, being raised from seed sown in January. With one or two exceptions they bear single flowers. Other cultivars are now available which produce semi-double and double flowers and yet more which have variegated foliage. Cultivation of these Semperflorens begonias is more difficult; seed is not normally available and they are usually grown as individual specimen pot plants, being propagated by basal cuttings. The following represent a few selected cultivars:

'Ballet' — white double flowers set off against bronze foliage — a strong grower and very floriferous.
'Lucy Locket' — bright pink double flowers — foliage green-bronze.
'Winkie' — rose-red double flowers — an everblooming, compact plant.
'Ernest K' — rose-red blooms attractively displayed against very deep-coloured foliage.

Included in this group of Semperflorens begonias which produce semi-double and double flowers there are a number referred to as 'Thimble Hybrids'. The deep thimble-shaped flowers are crested as the central stamens partially develop the characteristics of petals. This provides a vivid colour contrast to the flower. Several worth noting are:

'Goldilocks' — pink outer petals with golden yellow coloration in the thimble. Foliage light bronze.
'Firefly' — coral-red flowers with crested yellow centres — dark bronze foliage.
'Pistachio' — a dwarf grower — pink outer petals with crest that changes colour from green to yellow.
'Cinderella' — pink blooms with cherry red tips — yellow crest.

The variegated foliage Semperflorens begonias in general produce single-flowered blooms, their attraction being the calla lily-type leaves. Not surprisingly the name calla figures largely in the cultivar names.

'Calla King' — single white flowers — large green leaves flecked with white.
'Calla Lily' — an old variety with pink flowers. Leaves green at the base, paling to white at the tips.
'Calla Queen' — young plants are green, but with maturity white leaves are produced — single flowers in rose-pink.

'Charm' — cream and gold patches on green leaves — pale
pink flowers.

The Semperflorens group of begonias is a very rewarding one
requiring reasonable light conditions and temperatures of about
55-60°F (13-16°C) to produce a multitude of blooms the year
round. It should be remembered that while a number of the
above cultivars have been bred for pot plant use it is possible to
use any of the Semperflorens Cultorum group in this way. Once
the plant is growing strongly the tips should be removed to
encourage branching

Begonias Grown For Their Foliage

This is a very large group of begonias to which an entire book
could well be devoted. Here, however, it is possible only to
draw attention to a small selection of subjects, the choice of
which is quite arbitrary and personal. As we have already
noted, some of the begonias discussed below will also produce
quite showy flowers in addition to the most attractive foliage
but that may be considered to be a bonus. All the plants listed
here must be considered as greenhouse subjects, at least in
Great Britain and Europe though in certain areas of the USA a
number may spend part of the year out of doors.

Almost all of these begonias will require some degree of
heating during the winter months. Some may be successfully
grown in the home.

Four groups of begonias have been chosen for discussion;
namely, cane-stemmed begonias, shrub-like, rex begonias and
rhizomatous begonias. While this selection is not exhaustive
nevertheless it does present a fairly representative picture of the
potential offered by this group of plants.

Cane-stemmed Begonias

This group of begonias is one in which the purely arbitrary
division of growing for flowers versus growing for foliage is
perhaps at its most suspect. Nevertheless, outside the flowering
period it is the beauty and variety of the lovely foliage which is
the added attraction of this group. There is little doubt,
however, that the cane-stemmed begonias could be included in
either group, since so many of them are most attractive plants,
with or without flowers.

Cane-stemmed begonias are relatively easy to grow and,

especially in the case of the hybrids, will often reward the grower with a spectacular display of colour. The small florets appear like bunches of grapes 30-40 at one time and in colours which range from white through yellow to pink and red. It is not unusual to sub-divide this type of begonia on the basis of the leaf shape. Angel-wing begonias are so called because of the similarity of the leaf shape to the traditional angel wing. The leaf colour may range from light green to bronze and may be either plain or spotted silver. Superba begonias have distinctly different foliage in that the leaves are deeply incised but often silver spotted or splashed. This group tends to be a tall-growing one and careful pruning is called for to keep them manageable. The Mallet type of cane-stemmed begonias may be recognised by their mahogany red foliage frequently covered in red hairs.

Figure 2.2 An 'Angel wing' Begonia

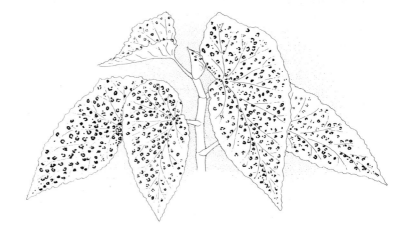

Though it is usual to stake the stems and grow them erect, a number of cane-stemmed begonias may be useful subjects for hanging baskets.

The male flowers usually open first and have often fallen from the plant before the females open. Most cane-stemmed begonias flower seasonally though a few can be persuaded to bloom the year round. The main growing season is from early spring to late autumn and to be at their best they require the night-time temperature not to fall below 60°F (16°C).

A select number of species and cultivars will be described separately.

B. albo-picta and *B. albo-picta rosea* — this Brazilian species can reach a height of 2ft — it has a slightly drooping habit and is heavily branched. The foliage is green and narrow and silver spotted — greenish-white flowers.

B. coccinea — another Brazilian species which can attain a height of 10ft, it has smooth green angel wing leaves with rather weak stems. The bright red flowers may be seen throughout the year. The species has been important in the development of the modern hybrids and was used in the parentage of B. Lucerna.

B. maculata — the first of the spotted leaf begonias to be introduced into Europe. The dull, dark green leaves are lobed and the pink flowers produced in summer. A variety of this angel wing begonia known as 'Wightii' has slightly larger flowers and more silver spotting on the leaves.

B. compta — a tall upright-growing plant with large angel wing leaves, grey-green with a satiny surface and striking silvery veins. The flowers are small and white in colour. It has been reported that it is difficult to root cuttings of this species.

B. angularis — sometimes listed as *B. zebrina* — long pointed grey-green leaves 7in × 3¹⁄4in with greyish-white veins and wavy edges. The small white flowers are borne in clusters. Can grow up to 3ft in height with thin angular stems; grows best in good light, but needs shade from direct sunlight.

B. dichroa — sweetly scented Brazilian species with a low growing spreading tendency. Glossy green leaves and large orange flowers are carried on short stems. Needs to be kept warm if bud drop is to be avoided. Almost all the orange cane-stemmed cultivars have *B. dichroa* in their parentage.

B. lubbersii — another sweet scented species. The satiny green leaves, which are red underneath, are joined at their centres to the stalk, i.e. they are peltate, and are pointed at both ends. Rarely exceeds 2ft when pot grown — pinkish white flowers in autumn and winter.

B. aconitifolia — can grow to 5ft, with limited branching. The leaves are dark green, splashed with silver, and are deeply incised and lobed. The flowers are white, tinted pink. This is one of the parents of the Superba hybrids.

B. sceptrum — like *B. aconitifolia* the base of the stems is swollen almost like a tuberous type, and the new canes appear from these swollen areas. The leaves are deeply cut, have a velvet texture and are slightly splashed with silver. The flowers are pale pink.

Numerous hybrids have been produced over the years of which only a small selection will be given here.

B. Argenteo-guttata — the name means silver spotted — a seedling from *B. albo-picta* which has retained the silver

25

spots of the parent. Has a bushy habit and makes a plant 2-2$\frac{1}{2}$ft high. Leaves are dark green 5$\frac{1}{2}$in × 2$\frac{1}{2}$in, slightly lobed and tinged with red on the underside. The white flowers hang in panicles. This plant will lose all its leaves in winter if the temperature falls below 50°F (10°C), but wil revive in spring unless it has been kept too wet in its semi-dormant condition. Sometimes known as the 'trout leaved begonia', occasionally this begonia is classed with the shrub-like group.

B. 'Florence Rita' — a cross of B. 'Orange Rubra' and *B. lubbersii* — grows 2-3ft high with leaves 10in × 3in, mid-green with silvery spots and reddish on the reverse. The leaves are partially peltate, the petiole joining the leaf about three quarters along the length of the axis. The upper end of the leaf is rounded and the lower end tapers to a point. The flowers are carried in panicles some 8-10in across.

B. 'Lubor' — another cross identical to the previous cultivar. The leaves are pointed at both ends with numerous silver spots decorating the satiny olive-green surface.

B. 'Lucerna' — a very popular cultivar more correctly named B. 'Corallina de Lucerna', it is a cross between *B. teuscheri* and *B. coccinea* and is often confused with another cane-stemmed cultivar B. 'President Carnot' (a cross of *B. olbia* with *B. teuscheri*). The plant is tall growing and has shiny dark green leaves heavily spotted with silver. The reverse side of the leaves are red, becoming green where the veins reach the leaf edges. Rose-pink flowers in large panicles mainly during late spring and summer. B.'Lucerna' does not like to be pot-bound.

B. 'Di-Anna' — a cross of *B. dichroa* and *B. coccinea*, the foliage is mid-green and heavily spotted with silver. This cultivar is free flowering, the blooms being salmon-orange.

B. 'Di-Erna' — similar cross to the previous cultivar except that the flowers are deep coral and the leaves do not have the silver spotting.

B. 'Orange Rubra' — a dichroa cross with B. 'Coral Rubra' — can attain a height of 2-3ft and has large, pale green leaves, occasionally with white spots that disappear with age. The flowers are orange in colour.

B. 'Pickobeth' — a *B. dregei* cross with B. Laura Englebert, this cultivar makes a most compact angel wing plant. The young leaves are bronze-green in colour becoming jade-green with age and decorated with cream spots. The leaves measure some 8in × 3¹₂in and are slightly lobed. The flowers are shocking pink with yellow stigma.

B. 'Flo'Belle Moseley' — similar cross to the previous cultivar. The leaves are deep mahogany, speckled white, and slightly waved. The flowers are pink in colour and the plant requires fairly high light levels.

B. 'Tom Ment' — yet another dichroa offspring as evidenced by the mandarin orange flowers. Large mid-green leaves silver or cream spotted and slightly waved. A very compact grower and almost a continual bloomer — could be very useful in a hanging basket.

B. 'Sophie Cecile' — a Superba type cane-stemmed hybrid with *B. sceptrum* in its parentage. Masses of pink flowers are set against deeply lobed green leaves splashed with silver. Requires very high light levels for best results.

B. 'Irene Nuss' — another Superba hybrid — very large clusters of coral pink flowers with velvety green foliage.

B. 'Tingley Mallet' — a Mallet type cane-stemmed begonia — deep red-bronze leaves spotted with silver-cream and covered with red hairs. Intermittent flushes of rose-pink flowers.

B. 'Gloire de Jouy' — another Mallet hybrid with silvery spotted round, green leaves which are red on the underside. The flowers are soft pink.

B. 'Margueritacea' — a compact growing Mallet hybrid with deep metallic purple leaves and pink flowers.

Shrub-like Begonias

Begonias included in this group tend to produce bushy plants with many basal growths. They vary considerably in height ranging from dwarf plants to those attaining 4ft or more. In a number of instances individual members of this group may produce quite attractive flowers, but the major interest lies in the very varied foliage colours and textures. Leaf sizes can be from 1in up to 12in or more and the surface may be glossy or matt. Leaves may be bare or they may be covered with tiny hairs — when the hairy covering is extensive the leaf is referred to as felted. In general they are very tolerant subjects which will grow well in a temperature of 63°F (17°C) and in good light conditions. An atmospheric humidty of about 50 per cent is adequate for their good health.

It is only possible to select a few species and cultivars from this large group of begonias, second in size only to the

27

rhizomatous group.

B. *bradei* — a Brazilian species discovered in 1953, it can grow
to 2ft and has soft, narrow, velvet green leaves $4^1\!2$in $\times$ $2^1\!2$in
and lined with red. The flowers are white.

B. *epipsila* — a very low growing Brazilian species with
thickened, leathery leaves which are dark glossy green on the
upper surface and with long, red-brown hairs on the
underside. The flowers, which are produced in the spring,
are small and white. This plant needs to be kept fairly dry in
the winter.

B. *foliosa* — probably the begonia with the smallest leaves, $^3\!4$in
$\times$ $^3\!8$in and elliptical in shape. It is frequently called the 'fern
begonia'. The stems may reach 2ft in length and bear minute
white flowers. This species needs warm conditions, e.g. 55-
60°F (13-16°C) and a high humidity.

B. *fuchsioides* — another small-leaved begonia with long stems.
The leaves are a glossy mid-green. The flowers are fuchsia-
like in red or pink shades and have a drooping habit.

B. *haageana* — known better in the USA as *B. scharffii*. It is a
hirsute begonia with large, soft olive-green leaves, red on the
reverse. Well grown specimens may attain 6ft in height. The
flowers are white, with small red hairs, and may be produced
throughout the year. Propagation of this species is by
cuttings, but it is essential that there is an axillary bud in the
leaf axil otherwise the propagated plant may fail to branch.

B. *hispida cucullifera* — a species which has large, lobed, soft,
velvety light-green leaves which carry adventitious leaflets
along the veins.

B. *incarnata* — a Brazilian species the foliage of which is palm-
like. Each leaf is divided into eight or ten 'fingers'.
Specimens can grow up to 6ft high and, if the growing tip is
removed the plant may die. Flowers are very small and
white.

B. *metallica* — a tall growing, well branched Mexican species
with medium-sized, dark green leaves (6in $\times$ $3^1\!2$in) which
have a metallic sheen. The leaves are covered with fine white
hairs and have dark veins. The flowers are pink.

B. *nitida* — could have been the first begonia introduced into
Britain in 1777 from Jamaica. It has broad, fleshy, glossy
green leaves which are slightly cup shaped. This species can
grow to 3ft in height and has small white and pink flowers in
winter. A different form *B. nitida odorata* has a slight
perfume detectable in the early morning.

B. *serripetala* — a New Guinean species with strikingly dark
copper-coloured foliage. The leaves (6in $\times$ $2^1\!2$in) are deeply

incised and undulating, the upper surface of which is covered with raised red spots. The flowers are deep pink and red. Plants may be grown upright to about 2ft in height or in hanging baskets. This species propagates readily from stem cuttings.

B. vitichoma — a Brazilian species which grows to 2ft in height. The light green leaves develop small tufts or growths on their surface. The flowers are white.

B. lindeneana (syn. *B. cubensis*) — a Cuban species which grows upright to 4ft in height. It has light green hairy leaves and bunches of white flowers.

B. olsoniae — a most attractive Brazilian species of compact habit, it has very lush, satiny-green leaves which are rounded with prominent ivory-coloured veining. The flowers are pale pink.

B. venosa — yet another Brazilian species which frequently grows as a single-stemmed plant. The leaves are very succulent, silvery-green in colour and felted with white hairs. The flowers are white and slightly spice scented. Propagation is by tip cuttings.

B. sanguinea — small white flowers but thick, mid-green, glossy leaves, blood-red on the reverse — an excellent species.

Of the many cultivars in this group the following are worthy of attention:

B. Alleryi — This is a French cultivar from 1904 using *B. metallica* and *B. gigantea* as parents. It is very similar to *B. metallica* but much more vigorous. The hairy leaves have purple veining and toothed edges. Throughout the year it carries pinkish-white flowers which are bearded.

B. Bavaria (B. Bayern) — this is reported to be a cross of German origin but the parentage is unknown. The plant has cane-like stems and small, pointed leaves sometimes silver spotted. The young leaves are reddish in colour. When grown in strong light the small flowers are deep red and when given a temperature of 50°F (10°C) it will bloom the year round. The plant height rarely exceeds 18in. It is useful for hanging baskets.

B. Preussen — probably from the same cross as B. Bavaria, grown at Kew under the name 'Thimotei', it is a dwarf growing plant with small pointed leaves and pink flowers. Some of the leaves carry faint white spots.

B. Corbeille de Feu — a Lemoine cross of 1891 using *B. semperflorens* and *B. fuchsioides*. It carries many flame-red flowers on upright stems. The leaves which are glossy green are oval and $3\frac{3}{4}$in × 2in. This cultivar may be grown out of doors where it will make a plant of some 2ft high but will not stand cold weather.

B. Druryi — a smooth, dark green leaved plant, the foliage being covered with red-brown hairs and red on the reverse. The flowers are red bearded and white in colour.

B. Ingramii — a cross of *B. nitida* and *B. fuchsioides*, this is an upright plant with small, serrated leaves, green in colour. It has deep pink flowers and will tolerate a lot of sun.

B. Richmondensis — very similar to B. Catalina which is another B. Digswelliana hybrid. It has shiny green leaves $4\frac{1}{4}$in × 24in and the flowers, produced the year round, are pink. It can grow to 2ft in height.

B. Thurstonii — an old favourite. The leaves are a metallic green and the flowers pink. Though an easy plant to grow it does need to have the growing tip pinched out to encourage the formation of a bushy plant.

B. Calico Kew — an easy grower with large, broad, deep green leaves speckled with coppery and green tones. The small, rose-pink flowers are carried above the foliage.

Rex Cultorum Group

This quite considerable group of begonias is grown entirely for the often spectacular foliage. Though of course flowers are produced they are often very insignificant and usually produced sporadically. Many growers remove the growing flower spikes before they rise above the foliage. All of this group have their true origins in the species *B. rex* but considerable hybridisation has been undertaken with many African and South American species. By far the greatest number of hybrids are rhizomatous though a small proportion do not produce rhizomes. The B. Rex Cultorum group can have small, medium or large leaves and the ornamental foliage may be highly coloured with shades of silver, green, red and purple etc. Often the leaf surfaces have a 'hammered' or pustular finish.

A number of cultivars are even more attractive because the basal lobes of the leaves overlap giving a spiral effect.

Begonias of this group have become very popular as houseplants and, as a result, many thousands of unnamed cultivars have been sold to the domestic market through supermarkets and garden centres. Nevertheless, specially selected and named cultivars are available, a few of which are listed below. Plants can be raised from seed, but it is well to remember that since the parents are hybrids then the offspring will not come true.

B. 'Fireflush' — a much sought after Rex with dark green leaves edged with black. The whole leaf surface is covered with fine red hairs. The new leaves contrast sharply having the appearance of red velvet.

B. 'Curly Fireflush' — this is a spiralled-leaf version of the previous cultivar.

B. 'Merry Christmas' — the leaves are a satiny carmine-red with a broad margin of bright green. The centre veins are deep purple.

B. 'Silver Queen' — soft silver pustular leaf with a trace of metallic purple in the centre overlaying the silver.

B. 'Silver King' — a silver leaf with contrasting green veins.

B. 'Queen of Hanover' — leaves are covered with bands of dark and light green and with silver markings. The leaf surface is covered with fine pink hairs.

B. 'Filigree' — laciniated leaves in bronze-green spotted with rose-pink and inlaid with satin-black.

B. 'Captain Nemo' — a spiralled silver leaf with edge margins in bright green.

B. 'Curly Merry Christmas' — a spiralled leaf with purple centre, satiny-red with bright green outline.

B. 'Lavender Glow' — leaves are silver coloured overlaid with scarlet and a jet black centre.

B. 'My Valentine' — a spiralled leaf in pale green with a heart-shaped centre of pink and rose-red.

B. 'Venetian Red' — the new leaves are silver becoming satin-red as they mature. The deep coloured veins contrast sharply with the leaf colour.

Rhizomatous Group

This is quite the largest group of begonias presently being grown. Though flowers are produced, undoubtedly the major attraction of this group is the foliage. In Britain the majority of available cultivars have *B. bowerae* (the 'eyelash' begonia) in the parentage and this seems to give rise to the dark-coloured tracery over the leaves. Some of the cultivars are also known as Tiger begonias. Other species, e.g. *B. conchifolia, B. pustulata, B. daedalea, B. mazae* and *B. carrieae*, have also been used in hybridising. With such a large group to choose from only a few examples of species and cultivars can be given here.

B. bowerae — the small 2in leaves are light green in colour and attractively marked with chocolate-brown tracery. The rhizome tends to grow erect and the leaves have hairs at the margins.

B. bowerae nigramarga — this species, also from Mexico, is a miniature form of the above.

B. conchifolia — this is a Mexican species with leaves resembling the nasturtium. The leaves are slightly peltate and twisted. The flowers are pale pink.

B. manicata — another Mexican species with upright rhizomes. The large leaves are smooth and green. The pink flowers are held above the foliage in spring.

B. manicata 'Aureo Crispa' — the light green leaves have yellow marbling and crinkled edges.

B. burle marx — a Brazilian species which can attain a height of 2ft. Has large, pustulate leaves in greenish-brown with a red sinus. The white flowers are held high above the foliage.

B. carrieae — a fairly recently discovered Mexican species with large, thick green leaves which are lobed. The white flowers are produced during winter.

B. paulensis — a Brazilian species with large, shiny, mid-green leaves. The intricate pattern of main and secondary veins gives the whole leaf a spider's web appearance.

B. 'Aquarius' — a Norah Bedson cross it grows to about 8in in height and has dark, velvety brown leaves. It produces pink flowers in the spring.

B. 'Beatrice Hadrell' — a *B. bowerae* with *B. heracleifolia* 'Sunderbruchii' hybrid it has small, star-shaped leaves where the green centre veins contrast sharply with the dark leaf colour. The pink flowers are produced in the early spring.

B. 'Black Prince' — very dark green serrated leaves with a lighter green petiole.

B. 'Cleopatra' — a dwarf plant with yellow and brown serrated leaves.

B. 'Chantilly Lace' — pale green leaves with fine black stitching. The flowers are white.

B. 'Norah Bedson' — mottled green 2in leaves with chocolate markings — fine edging in white and speckled red stems.

B. 'Mac's Gold' — miniature leaves, pointed, star-shaped and lobed, red-brown in colour with green margin and petiole.

B. 'Red Spider' — small green leaves with distinctive red veins and sinus.

B. 'Scherzo' — very pronounced yellow serrated leaves with black markings.

B. 'Red Planet' — small green leaves very heavily mottled with deep red colouration.

B. 'Skeezar' — silver and green leaves, and greenish-white

flowers.

B. 'Universe' — a cross of 'Norah Bedson' with 'Leslie Lynn'. The maple-shaped leaves are bright green with maroon-red mottling.

B. 'Sun God' — this is a cross of *B. bowerae* with B. Zip, the latter being a select form of *B. conchifolia*. The plant is compact and has glossy, nasturtium-like leaves with a red sinus and red underneath.

B. Feastii Helix (syn. Erythrophylla Helix) — this cultivar has plain green spiral leaves and produces pink flowers in the spring. It is a sport of the plain-leaved B. Erythrophylla.

CHAPTER 3

Cultivation of Begonias

In the temperate zones of Britain, Europe and much of the USA the spring and autumn temperatures are inadequate to maintain the necessary growth of almost the entire Begoniaceae family and winter temperatures are too low for the survival of any begonia. In a few areas of the USA it may well be possible to grow and flower a large number of begonias out of doors.

In Britain and Europe it is the normal practice to start tuberous double begonias and semperflorens intended for garden work in a protected environment and then to transfer them out of doors when all danger of frost has passed. All the cane-stemmed types, rhizomatous, Rex cultorum etc. are grown in greenhouses or conservatories or as houseplants. The large-flowered tuberous double begonias are grown in greenhouses if their maximum potential is to be realised.

Tuberous double begonias do not mix very well with other subjects, preferring shade and high humidity; therefore, if at all possible, it is desirable to dedicate a greenhouse entirely to their cultivation.

The Greenhouse

The choice between a metal-framed structure and a timber frame is entirely personal. Certainly a timber frame requires much more maintenance and in this respect there are advantages in the use of cedar wood. Since begonias are usually grown as pot plants a plant house on dwarf walls (2ft 6in high) is ideal, especially as this structure will retain heat better in the early and late season. A well grown mature tuberous double begonia may attain a height of 3-3$\frac{1}{2}$ft above the rim of the pot and this should be borne in mind with respect to the height of the eaves. Such an adult plant could also have a diameter of some 3ft or more and this should be an additional consideration. For instance, should the greenhouse have vertical or inclined sides; is the door width adequate for the movement of such large plants? The experience of countless growers is universally the same; i.e. always purchase the largest greenhouse which you can afford and try to ensure the greatest amount of headroom.

The major problem which most growers of tuberous double begonias experience is how to keep the temperature down in the summer months rather than how to maintain high temperatures during the winter; to this end it is absolutely essential that adequate ventilation is available. It is not unusual for growers to insist on having a door at each end of the greenhouse, while others provide for the easy removal of glass panes. Sliding ventilators at low levels can be beneficial and 12in extractor fans in the upper section of the gable end can be very useful at the height of summer. As a general guide it should be said that in a normal season in Britain it should not be necessary to close the doors or ventilators of the greenhouse from about May until late August.

The question of solid benches versus the slatted type is a very vexed one. Certainly solid benches covered with gravel or Hortag (a highly absorbent inert aggregate) and well supplied with water, can help a lot towards providing the atmospheric humidity required for good cultivation. On the other hand, slatted benches do assist in ensuring good air circulation, also important to the well being of begonias. One problem with the solid benches is that they require a very vigorous hygiene programme if disease problems are not to get out of hand.

Greenhouse heating is yet another issue over which argument can generate much of its own heat. For the growers of the large-flowered tuberous double begonias it is perfectly feasible to be successful with no heat at all or at least with a minimum amount in the late autumn. This of course means starting tubers as late as March-April in Britain (early-mid spring) and accepting a short flowering season, say August-September (late summer). If this sort of restriction is acceptable, then an open blue-flame paraffin or a natural gas heater is probably adequate. The experience of many growers is, however, that when heat is needed in the early part of the year, e.g. February, then this type of heater can bring severe cultural problems with young plants and particularly with the foliage of the paler coloured cultivars such as 'Judy Langdon', 'Sweet Dreams' etc. Of course those who grow the type of begonia which does not have a dormant period will experience similar difficulties unless adequate ventilation is provided, and this rather defeats the object. If liquid fuels must be used then it is far better to use an indirect system where the heat source is outside the greenhouse and is used to provide hot water which is then pump circulated through alloy pipes.

Electrical heating is very convenient either in the form of hot air blowers or tubular heaters. Though this form of heating is probably more expensive per unit than other energy sources the capital outlay is often less and the control of temperature by the use of thermostats is both easy and accurate. The availability of electricity in the greenhouse is a great asset since it may be used for lighting and for propagation; incorrectly installed, however, it can be lethal. Professional advice should always be sought and taken on the safe use of electricity in the greenhouse.

It is of great benefit to have mains water piped into the greenhouse and, with the ready availability of plastic fittings, such an installation need no longer be expensive. Mains water on site may be used for plant propagation and for humidifying the greenhouse atmosphere. Though many growers succeed well enough without the luxury of humidification it can be a boon in the height of a hot summer. Misting nozzles placed at 4ft intervals underneath the benches and operated by a simple mains solenoid valve can be easily triggered by a time-clock. The intervals between spraying can be varied to suit the atmospheric conditions. It is very questionable whether emptying the occasional two gallons of water over the greenhouse floor (euphemistically called 'damping down') in the height of a hot summer does any real good at all. If the grower intends to raise the atmospheric humidity then this must be done on a greater scale and much more frequently. One practical step which can be taken is to lay polythene sheeting below the benches and to cover this with a 2in depth of $\frac{1}{4}$in-$\frac{1}{2}$in gravel. The polythene will greatly assist in retaining the water from either the misting or the 'damping down' procedures.

Begonias are naturally shade loving plants and the majority of subjects do not thrive in full sun. Tuberous double begonias, even in the early spring, are rapidly scorched when exposed to the sun's rays. In Britain some form of shading is required from about late March right through to September/October. The usual method is to apply a wash of diluted white emulsion paint (one part to eight parts water) to the outside of the glass. Alternatively one of the commercial shading washes can be used. A much better method, however, is to fasten one of the synthetic fabric shade cloths to the outside of the greenhouse and at about 4in from the glass. This gap helps to ensure a cooling stream of air passing across the glass. These shade cloths can be obtained in various grades according to the amount of light which passes through — the 50 per cent grade is adequate for begonia cultivation. The modern shade cloth will stand up to many years of exposure to the elements. This is not always the case with the continuous film type of shading which often disintegrates after the second year of use.

And, finally, siting the greenhouse — so often this is dictated by issues other than mere horticulture, but whenever possible the structure should be placed so that the ridge bar is in an east-west direction; in this way it is probably necessary only to shade one side of the greenhouse.

Every dedicated grower of begonias, or any other plant for that matter, will have his or her own personal method of cultivation, methods which have been modified by years of success or failure. In this book there is no intention to woo growers away from their individual cultivation methods, but rather to get the new and novice growers off to a good start. Later on they, too, might begin to experiment in order to develop the optimum conditions for their own growing techniques. It would clearly be impossible in a book of this size to deal exhaustively with the detailed cultivation of the many different types of begonia grown today. Special emphasis has therefore been given to the cultivation of tuberous double begonias and only general guidelines for other members of the begonia family.

Tuberous begonias may be grown from seed or from tubers. Certainly growing from seed may well be the cheapest way to obtain a stock of begonias, but it is usual to adopt this approach only when the objective is to provide garden bedding plants. It will also take two years to achieve the maximum plant potential, whereas growing from tubers allows this to be realised in the first year though the capital outlay will be much greater. For greenhouse work the very best results can only be obtained from selected tubers. The methods described below are applicable to all begonias which produce tubers, i.e. large-flowered doubles, cascades, multifloras, 'non-stops' etc. and, in the case of growing from seed, will apply to all types of begonia which will produce viable seed.

Tuberous Double Begonias

From Seed

The essentials for seed raising are good seed, a heated propagator, a light open compost and a lot of patience! With these requirements met it should be possible to raise a batch of seedlings with little more difficulty than a batch of any other annual bedding plant. Good quality seed is essential if a high proportion of double flowers is sought and it is therefore recommended that it should be purchased from a firm specialising in begonias. Tuberous double begonia seed may be purchased either in mixed colours or in six or eight individual colours as well as Pendula mixed.

Begonia seed is extremely small (about 50,000 per gram), so take great care when opening the packet. A 5in diameter half pot or pan is large enough to accommodate the seedlings from a single packet. A few crocks or popcorn-sized pieces of foamed polystyrene placed in the pots will ensure adequate drainage. The pot should now be filled with moist seed compost which is then gently firmed but not compacted. The compost may be either a good quality John Innes seed compost (loam based) or one of the soilless types. The John Innes compost may be purchased locally or made up according to the formula:

2 parts by volume of sterilised loam
1 part by volume of fine sphagnum moss peat
1 part by volume of dry silver sand

The first two of these ingredients must be passed through a $\frac{1}{8}$in mesh sieve. Ideally the loam should be sterilised, but in the absence of suitable equipment satisfactory results may be obtained using the chemical Basamid (Dazomet). This material can irritate the nose and mouth, so the instructions for use should be carefully observed. To each 8 gallons (4 bucketsful) of this mix is added:

$1\frac{1}{2}$oz (43g) superphosphate of lime
$\frac{3}{8}$oz ($10\frac{1}{2}$g) ground chalk (carbonate of lime)

To obtain a uniform distribution of the fertiliser mix it first with the silver sand before adding the loam and peat. Since the quality of loam and loam based composts has deteriorated during the past decade there is much to be gained from using the peat based composts which are generally of a much more uniform quality.

A simple peat based compost can readily be prepared by mixing:

3 × 2gal. of sphagnum moss peat
1 × 2gal. of silver sand

Again the peat should be passed through a sieve of $\frac{1}{8}$in mesh. To this mixture now add either the recommended amount of a proprietary seed compost base or:

1oz (28g) superphosphate of lime
3oz (85g) of any granular balanced fertiliser

38

If the compost is intended for transplanting seedlings then it should also contain, in addition to the above:

1oz (28g) dolomite magnesium ground limestone.

The compost can now be watered from above, using a fine rose on the watering can, and then left to drain for about 30 minutes. The begonia seed should now be admixed with about twice its volume of dry silver sand and then sprinkled uniformly over the surface of the compost. The added sand will ensure a more uniform distribution of the seed. After sowing, the seed should not be covered since the germination of begonias will occur only in the light. Then place the pot or pan in an electrically heated propagator maintained at 65-70°F (18-21°C). Germination, which may take from eight to ten days (though in the case of certain species much longer), appears to be more successful when the atmosphere is moist and warm. These conditions may be readily achieved by first placing trays containing a $\frac{1}{2}$in deep layer of wet gravel in the propagator. The seed pans are placed on this gravel and the trays closed using clear plastic domes, each of which is ventilated. The warm, humid microenvironment thus produced is also ideal for the growth of fungus spores, e.g. pythium, which will cause 'damping off' when the seed germinates. The likelihood of a fungal attack may be considerably reduced by including a small amount of fungicide, e.g. orthocide or propamocarb (Filex), in the water used to moisten the gravel. For the successful rearing of seedlings it is vital that the surface of the compost is never allowed to dry out; this may be prevented by daily misting with water containing fungicide. The siting of the propagator is not unimportant since, while it must not be placed in a dark corner, it must also be kept out of direct sunlight. The first green leaves should appear within about 5-6 days and at this stage great care should be taken with the daily misting. From this stage the seedlings should make steady growth for the next 3-4 weeks when it will be necessary to transplant into fresh compost. Begonia seedlings seem to suffer less check to their growth when this first transplanting is done early, i.e. when the first true leaf has formed. A soilless compost is preferable for this stage of cultivation — again it should be gently firmed, watered from above and allowed to drain. A convenient method of transplanting which prevents undue bruising of the fleshy, fragile stems is to use two small alloy plant labels, one of which has a slot cut into it at the tapered end. Taking the uncut label in one hand the point is pushed under the seedling to lever it up and, with the slotted label in the other hand, the slot is positioned under the lower leaves. It should now be possible to lift the seedling and drop it into a small hole in the new compost made by the pointed end of the uncut label.

The seedlings should be planted about ³₄in-1in apart which will give about 130 to 150 in a normal seed tray. The tray should

Figure 3.1 The Wrong Way to Sow Seeds

Figure 3.2 Propagator Showing Gravel Trays and Plastic Covers Creating a Humid Microenvironment

be placed in the propagator at 65-70°F (18-21°C) and again the compost must never dry out. Whenever watering is required it must be done by immersing the tray in water and not by overhead application. A second transplanting will be required as the seedlings continue to grow — this should be in about five to six weeks. The same compost is used but now the plantlets need to be spaced some 2in apart. It is at this stage that growing space is at a premium. As many trays as possible should be placed in the propagator and the excess will have to remain on the greenhouse staging at a lower temperature; of course the growth rate of these plants will slow down. Watering the plantlets from below will help to maintain dry leaves and a small addition of fungicide will greatly help to ward off attacks of pythium. By the end of April in Britain (mid-spring) there should be enough sunlight to maintain the greenhouse temperatures at about 55-60°F (13-16°C) and by this time all the seedlings should be on the staging.

Towards the end of May in Britain (late spring) preparations should be well advanced for the eventual bedding out of those seedlings destined for garden display. For these plants a two week hardening off period in a cold frame is necessary particularly to avoid sun scorch and the inevitable check to growth which would otherwise occur. An examination of the time schedule described above reveals that the begonia seed needs to be sown in early January (mid-late winter) if the resulting plants, bedded out in June (early summer), are to provide a colourful flower display in say, late July or early August (mid-late summer).

Those seedlings not intended for outdoor use may be potted up individually and grown on in the greenhouse. Their treatment will be identical to that given to the begonias grown from tubers for greenhouse use and will be dealt with on page 47.

The preparation of the outdoor bedding site and the further growing of the seedlings is dealt with on page 64.

From Tubers

Every spring in Britain hundreds of thousands of begonia tubers are sold through garden centres, nurseries, multiple stores and through mail order. The majority of these tubers are imported from Belgium and Holland and have been graded largely on the basis of flower colour and tuber size. By and large they are suitable for bedding displays, but they lack the quality and potential which is desirable in a greenhouse or exhibition plant.

Before embarking on the purchase of tubers it is, therefore, sensible to decide on the end product desired. If high quality plants and flowers are sought then once again it is the specialist nursery which should be approached. Named cultivars which have been carefully selected on the grounds of quality are moderately expensive though unnamed tubers which are only marginally inferior can be purchased at more modest cost. For the novice grower or beginner who has not yet established whether he or she can achieve the optimum growing conditions it would be sensible to start with the latter type of tuber before embarking on a large financial outlay.

Naturally the decision as to which quality to purchase must also be influenced by the question of where the plants are to be grown. The named cultivars and the unnamed exhibition quality tubers will most probably be grown in a greenhouse or conservatory where protection from the weather will help the grower to achieve much higher standards of cultivation. The less expensive tubers will certainly be used for outdoor display. Greenhouse cultivation will be considered first.

Greenhouse Cultivation

Top quality named and unnamed begonia tubers are usually in great demand and are rapidly sold out each year. It is best to place an order with the nursery during the late summer and autumn for delivery the following late winter (January or February in Britain). On receiving the dormant tubers they should be carefully examined for any sign of rot – this might be either hard or soft. Any excessively hard or soft tubers should be returned to the suppliers after acquainting them of the problem. Newcomers to begonia cultivation sometimes feel concerned about the often very variable sizes of the tubers on purchase. It must be realised that the original species involved in the breeding programmes might still affect tuber size, e.g. the yellow *B. pearcei* tends to confer small tuber size on its offspring. The important thing is that tubers should be two years old on purchase.

On receiving the tubers a decision has then to be made as to when to start the tubers into growth. As a guide, begonias will be grown for some six months before flowering and acceptable plant growth rates are achieved only with an air temperature of 60°F (16°C) during the day and 50°F (10°C) at night. Unless heat is available in the greenhouse it is unwise to start the tubers into growth before mid-March (early spring) though plants grown in this way will have a slightly shorter flowering season.

The tubers will need to be stored in a cool and fairly dry place until ready to start. The greenhouse is not the ideal storage place since the atmosphere is often quite humid and, though the night temperatures may be as low as 40°F (4.5°C), daytime temperatures may occasionally rise to 60-70°F (16-21°C). This combination of humidity and warmth might start them prematurely into growth.

If the greenhouse can be heated then tubers may be started in early January (mid-late winter) using a propagator able to maintain a temperature of 60-65°F (16-18°C). It must be remembered, however, that within a few weeks of starting, the tubers will need to be moved into the main greenhouse where the temperature should not fall below 50°F (10°C) and at this time of the year this can be an expensive luxury. Begonias started in this way will have a flowering season extended by some six weeks, though it must also be remembered that the later flowers will show some decrease in size over those at the beginning of the flowering season.

It is unnecessary for the starting compost to contain fertiliser and an open mixture of sphagnum peat and sharp sand or grit can be an ideal medium. As we shall observe later tuberous begonias prefer a growing medium which is only slightly acidic so it is better to add a small amount of ground limestone to the starting compost.

There is a school of thought which holds that the root system which develops in a soilless compost will not transplant well into a loam-based potting medium. Though the evidence for this assertion is very dubious it can be accommodated by simply starting the tubers in a 50/50 mix of loam and peat mixed in the correct proportion with grit. For adult tubers the ideal starting container is a deep-sided box (about $4\frac{1}{2}$in deep) and filled to 2in with compost. The tubers are laid on top of the compost (concave side uppermost) and then covered with a thin layer (about $\frac{3}{8}$in) of the medium. Completely covering the tubers brings two major advantages:

(a)   the capillary action of the medium effectively prevents water lodging in the crown of the tuber.

(b)   it encourages root formation over the entire surface of the tuber.

The correct labels are inserted, the compost watered so that it is uniformly moist, and the box placed in the heated propagator. The begonias will not start into growth at one and the same time so that eventually some will have to be removed while others remain in the propagator. In order to reduce to a minimum the possibility of root entanglement and hence

Figure 3.3 Tuberous Begonias in Starting Trays — Different Degrees of Development

damage, a good 2in space should be left between the tubers. From now on a careful watch should be kept on the tubers; first, to ensure that the compost is kept moist and second, to keep a check on the amount of root growth and the general health of the plants.

This period is a most critical one in the cultivation of tuberous begonias since it is the time when the ultimate amount of root growth will be determined. It is impossible to grow good begonias without first obtaining adequate root growth. Top growth at this stage of cultivation is of little or no consequence; in fact, in the absence of significant root development it would be a good principle to remove any stems which have reached 3in high and use them as cuttings. When a good potential root system has been obtained the tubers should be potted up individually even though top growth may only be ^{1}2-^{3}4in high. For the small cutting tubers (perhaps ^{1}2-1in in diameter) it is better to start them in individual pots using the same type of compost. Very occasionally an entire cutting tuber will be affected by brown rot which could so easily spread to the others if they were boxed up.

On being removed from the propagator the tubers are potted into pots; these should be 2in larger than the overall root system. The choice of compost is a very personal one and most of the experienced growers have their own idiosyncrasies in this respect. In the main, however, the composts are either peat-based soilless or loam-based John Innes types. Excellent results can be obtained from either type of medium though the loam-based are more difficult for the beginner. It is better to deal with the two components separately.

John Innes Composts. The first attempt to produce a consistent and scientifically based compost was made many years ago at the John Innes Institute and it met with considerable success. The basic formulation was sterilised loam, sphagnum peat and sand in volume ratio of 7:3:2. To this was added a balanced fertiliser and lime, the amount used determining whether the No. 1, 2, or 3 medium was being produced. This formulation, particularly the Nos. 2 and 3 may still be used with confidence, but it is questionable whether composts sold under this name and available through the normal outlets have been made in strict accordance with the original instructions. The usual procedure adopted for loam sterilisation is by steam heating and, while this might kill most insect pests and weeds, it often fails to eradicate eelworm and, in addition, heat sterilisation does appear to alter the physical structure of the loam. One very successful nursery in Britain found after many years of experience that it was far better to use a good quality loam (very difficult to obtain nowadays) cut 3-4in thick and stack it with old cow manure in the ratio 6:1 for at least nine months before use — the loam was unsterilised and this gave rise to a 'live compost'. For those growers who may still have access to good quality fibrous loam and wish to experiment with their own composts, sterilisation can now be successfully carried out chemically with such materials as Dazomet. Following the manufacturer's instructions chemical sterilisation can be most effective without adversely affecting the physical structure of the loam.

Two somewhat different formulations are suggested here, either of which growers might like to try.

1. 7 parts by volume of fibrous loam
   3 parts by volume sphagnum peat
   2 parts by volume $\frac{1}{8}$in sharp grit

These ingredients should be well mixed, the peat having been made slightly moist and the peat and loam having been passed through a $\frac{3}{8}$-$\frac{1}{2}$in mesh sieve. To this mixture must be added a source of calcium, usually in the form of ground chalk, and a well balanced fertiliser. The alternatives are:

(a)   6oz (170g) hoof and horn or 2oz (56g) Nitroform

    6oz (170g) superphosphate of lime
    3oz (85g) sulphate of potash
    3oz (85g) ground chalk

or

(b)   15oz (425g) John Innes Base Fertiliser
    3oz (85g) ground chalk

Many growers use the John Innes No. 2 mixture, i.e. the quantities in (a) or (b) mixed with 8 × 2gal. of the loam/peat/grit mixture for the first and final potting. Others use the No. 2 for first potting and No. 3 (increase the amounts of (a) or (b) by 50 per cent for the final potting).

2.   Another well tried formulation is:

    3 parts by volume fibrous loam
    1 part by volume leaf mould
    2 parts by volume sphagnum peat
    1 part by volume dried cow manure
    1 part by volume $\frac{1}{8}$in sharp grit

This mixture is also made up to the John Innes No. 2 or 3 formula by using (a) or (b) above in the correct proportion. One of the advantages of loam-based composts is that they are quite heavy and this helps to stabilise the larger plants against the very real danger of falling over. The more obvious disadvantages are that they require a stock of five or six different ingredients to be kept, and the quality of one or two of the components might differ widely from year to year.

Soilless Composts. During the past two decades there has been a marked move towards the replacement of loam-based growing media by the soilless types. These peat-based composts are readily available and it is possible to maintain a uniform standard in terms of compositions, quality and structure from year to year. These composts may be purchased ready for use or the individual ingredients can be bought for use by the DIY grower. One popular mix used by many growers is:

    3 parts by volume sphagnum peat

    or

    $2\frac{1}{2}$ parts by volume sphagnum peat and
    $\frac{1}{2}$ part by volume $\frac{1}{8}$in sharp grit

These are mixed thoroughly and to 8 × 2gal. of this mix add 28oz (794g) special base fertiliser. The peats used in this formula are usually quite acidic and it is therefore beneficial to add a small amount of ground chalk to the compost.

Some growers prefer to replace up to half of the grit with Perlite, an inert material of volcanic origin, and which can be purchased in a number of different grades. The disadvantage of this is that the stability of the pot plant is reduced. A reasonably well grown begonia in a 7in pot will be top heavy and will insist on falling over. Composts of this type should not be compacted; indeed it is only necessary to knock the pot on a firm, flat surface to settle the medium.

While there is no attempt to woo the confirmed loam-based grower over to the alternative compost there is no doubt that excellent plants can be grown in the peat-based media. For the novice grower the reproducibility of this type of compost reduces his or her problems by one and it becomes perfectly feasible to grow begonias well even in the first year. It is also important to note that the ingredients are sterile and therefore, by their use one is not importing soil borne diseases such as rots or eelworm.

Whatever type of compost is chosen by the grower it is vital that it is open and drains well for, like many other pot plant subjects, begonias will soon succumb to overwet root conditions.

Naturally there are growers who feel that they can get the best of both worlds by using a mixture of 2 parts of loam based to 1 part of soilless compost. It has to be said, however, that there seems to be no good reason for taking this approach. Having chosen a particular type of compost it is unwise to change the medium during the subsequent growing procedure. There does appear to be evidence that the root systems developed in the two composts are different.

First Potting

In the first potting the tuber should be placed so that its upper surface finishes 2-2½in below the rim of the pot, and covered with about ¾in of compost. As long as the compost is sufficiently moist there will be no need to water the pot at this stage and indeed overwatering now would be most detrimental to the continued health of the plant. At this stage most plants will have to be on the open staging and, as is usual in most amateurs' greenhouses this will probably mean low night temperatures, e.g. 40-50°F (4-10°C) in the early spring. Under these conditions growth will be very slow and it is important that overwatering does not happen since the plants cannot

Figure 3.4 An Adult
Tuber Ready for
Potting into a 10in
Pot

Figure 3.5 First
Potting

transpire very readily. In this respect plastic pots are a greater problem than clays. The pots should be well spaced on the bench and every encouragement given to good air circulation.

This is also the time (early spring) when greenhouse shading is required, whether a permanent wash applied to the glass or a shade cloth. Even though the sun's heat appears to be insufficient to do much damage the tender begonia foliage will be badly scorched inside the greenhouse unless protection is given. Extensive scorching will severely check growth.

The plants will remain in their first pots until the root system has developed to the point where it is beginning to run around the inside of the pot. This may take some four to six weeks, depending upon various factors such as plant vigour, temperature, growing skills etc. At this stage it will be necessary to move the plants on into their final flowering pots. It is a mistake to delay this until the first pot becomes full of root. If this is allowed to happen the root system does not seem able to penetrate the new compost, root development is held up or even prevented and the plant cannot achieve its full potential.

Figure 3.6 Ready for Final Potting

Final Potting

This final potting should be a move up two to three inches in pot size, i.e. small tubers, say, up to 1in in diameter may be flowered in 5-5$\frac{1}{2}$in pots, but the larger tubers will need an 8in pot.

Once again the choice between clay and plastic pots is a purely personal one. Certainly clay pots dry out much faster than the plastic type, but this could be a serious disadvantage during a hot spell especially for the grower who is unable to attend to the plants during the day. The tiny roots do adhere to clay pots much more tenaciously than to plastic surfaces and are more easily damaged when potting on — this is an argument for making the move in good time and not waiting until the pot is full of roots. The combination of soilless compost and plastic pots will make a very unstable pot plant when fully grown.

Figure 3.7 Final Potting — Room for Top Dressing

The final potting compost must be of the same type as that already used except that it will probably contain more base fertiliser, e.g. a John Innes No. 3 rather than No. 2. The surface of the old root ball must be placed at about 2$\frac{1}{2}$in below the rim of the new pot. Begonias are not deep-rooting plants and during the growing season many surface roots will appear. Each time this occurs a light top dressing should be applied to encourage further root growth. This should be continued until the compost surface is within 1in of the rim of the pot. Any further top

Figure 3.8 Tuberous
Double Begonia in
Need of 'Dressing'

dressing will make for difficult watering. Some growers incorporate a quick-acting high potash fertiliser into the later top dressing but this is quite unnecessary since it is better to attend to the needs of the plant through liquid feeding.

Plant Management

An essential feature of successful begonia pot plant culture is to prevent too many stems developing on a young tuber. When purchased, most tubers are two years old and at this age it would be wise to restrict the number of developing growths to one or two. Whenever possible these two stems should be at the same stage of growth, i.e. of the same height and of about the same vigour. Any excess basal growths should be removed when they are about $2\frac{1}{2}$in high and used as cuttings. With a two-stemmed plant it is desirable that all the flowers face generally in the same direction and this is more likely if the tips of the leaves also point generally in the same direction.

Disbudding

Very often begonias show a pronounced tendency to produce buds even when the plants are but a few inches high. All buds should be removed until the plant has been in its final pot for at

51

Figure 3.9 Begonia
'Dressed', Leaving
One Main Stem and
One Side-shoot

least six weeks or until there are at least four pairs of leaves on the main stem. When the buds are eventually allowed to develop it will be noted that they are produced in groups of three. The centre or male bud is flanked by two others (usually, but not exclusively, female) and it is the centre male bud which is allowed to flower. As soon as possible the two flanking buds are removed without damaging the flowering bud — this can most easily be done with a small pair of fine scissors.

Side-shoots

With a young tuber it is unwise to allow more than two side-shoots per stem to develop to flowering size. Indeed it is doubtful whether more than two would develop early enough to produce flowers at the same time as the main stems. Again it is better with a two-stemmed plant that the side-shoots also face in roughly the same direction as the main stem leaves — this simply means that all the flowers will be producd in an arc of some 120° when viewed from the front. Excess side-shoots may be removed and used as cuttings, but if they are not required for propagation it is better simply to remove their growing tips; in this way they will continue to provide foliage to the flowering plant.

52

Figure 3.10
Two-stemmed Plant
— the Flowers Will
be Produced in a
160° Arc

Watering

It is very difficult to state accurately just how often a begonia should be watered since this so much depends upon factors such as the type of compost, how compacted it is, the type and size of pot, atmospheric conditions etc. Perhaps it is in this one area of cultivation that a good grower can be differentiated from a not so good grower. Certainly a pot in which the compost has contracted away from the sides is urgently in need of water and a damp, waterlogged compost desperately requires drying out. Between these two extremes is a whole spectrum of need. Immediately after potting, very little water will be required and the plant should be allowed to settle for three or four days. On the other hand, when the final pots are full of roots and in warm weather, daily or even twice daily applications of water might be called for. Remember, however, that a wet compost should not be watered; this will simply expel air from the root system and without oxygen the roots will die. Very often a dry compost surface hides a wet medium further down the pot and here moisture meters can be useful. It is frequently possible to 'feel' the need for water by picking up the pot and judging its weight. In general begonias should be allowed to almost dry out between applications of water. Here the emphasis is on 'almost', since dry peat composts are very difficult to re-wet.

53

Careful observation of the foliage will indicate when a plant requires water since at this time there is often a slight paling of the leaves and the veins become more prominent. Applications of water should not be made after mid-afternoon, otherwise, with the evening temperature drop, the plants will find it difficult to transpire the moisture through the leaves. This usually results in beads of water standing on the leaf margins which could damage the blooms, especially when the plants are in bud or flower.

Feeding

Opinions on this aspect of cultivation (should one feed and if so with what, at what strength and how frequently?), are as diverse among growers of begonias as of almost every other type of plant. All plantsmen will surely agree, however, that excessive feeding just prior to flowering time will not correct for a season of poor growing technique nor is there some 'magic formulation' which will convert very mediocre blooms into show winners. In common with most other plant subjects, begonias will benefit from consistency in growing conditions throughout the season, i.e. a reasonably uniform daytime temperature, fairly constant light levels and humidity and a compost which is allowed to be neither dry nor waterlogged. In this context begonias will perform better if the nutrients necessary for healthy growth are also available at a fairly constant level. All the nutrients enter the plant through the root system and, if this is inadequate, then the plant can never attain its full potential no matter how much feeding is done. Plants grown in pots have a restricted root system compared to those grown in the open where the roots can continuously forage for nutrients. For a pot plant all that is required for growth must come from the atmosphere, the compost or from liquid feeds. In order that it might produce healthy stems, foliage, roots and flowers a plant must be provided with certain building blocks and sufficient daylight to carry out the necessary photosynthesis. These basic building blocks may be described in terms of some sixteen elements, some of which are needed in large amounts and are referred to as macronutrients, while others are required in very small quantities and are described as micronutrients. It should be noted that a very small deficiency in a micronutrient can have just as serious an effect on plant health as a much larger deficiency in a macronutrient.

The elements carbon, hydrogen and oxygen required in large

quantities by all plants are obtained from the atmosphere and from water, so will not be considered further. Nitrogen, phosphorous and potassium (refered to as the NPK elements) are the so-called macronutrients and most liquid feeds and fertilisers carry an analysis of these three elements in terms of the percentages available. Three elements needed in quantities somewhat less than the macronutrients but greater than the micronutrients are calcium, magnesium and sulphur.

The micronutrients are boron, chlorine, iron, molybdenum, zinc, copper and manganese and are needed only in parts per million. Many modern liquid feeds as well as healthy fibrous loam contain adequate amounts of the micronutrients, but when making up one's own soilless composts it is advisable to add 1_2oz (14g) of Trace Element Frit 253A to 8 gal. (1 bushel) of compost to ensure a sufficient level of these elements. The subject of nutrient balance in relationship to plant health is a complex one and beyond the scope of this present text, but the following points may be made concerning a few of the building blocks.

Phosphorous is an element vital to the proper development of the root system but its availability to the plant is closely allied to the levels of magnesium.

Potassium is the element which is important to the production of flowers, but, if present in excess, can create a magnesium deficiency which in turn will reduce the availability of phosphorous.

Nitrogen must be available throughout the growing season though an excess of this element will lead to soft cellular tissue thus rendering the plant more susceptible to fungal and bacterial attack.

Calcium has an important role in plant growth since it is the element which is vital to the formation and development of shoot tips and also assists in making nitrogen available to the plant. All these nutrients, macro and micro, must be available to the developing plant at all times, though the relative amounts of each might change slightly during the growing season. For the bulk of the growing period the macronutrients need to be supplied in roughly equal amounts. When the flowering season approaches it may well be beneficial to increase the potassium levels but to maintain a constant amount of nitrogen and phosphorous.

The macroelements NPK may be supplied in 'organic form', i.e. incorporated into the compost in the form of Hoof and Horn, bone-meal etc; in this case they need bacterial action to break them down into the form in which the plant can assimilate them. This is a relatively slow process. The bacteria involved require oxygen to function properly; hence the need for an open compost which is not waterlogged.

Alternatively the macronutrients may be supplied as a liquid feed and in an 'inorganic form' and are thus immediately available to the plant when watered into the pot. These proprietary fertilisers have an important auxiliary feeding part to play.

Most composts of both the loam-based and soilless types include macronutrients in the organic and the inorganic forms so that, on potting, the plants have the essential building blocks immediately available and there is no need to apply auxiliary fertilisers for a few weeks. Loam-based composts usually employ hoof and horn to supply slow release nitrogen, but phosphorous and potassium in inorganic form, the NPK ratio being roughly 10:15:20. A somewhat more rapid supply of nitrogen can be obtained by substituting Nitroform for the Hoof and Horn.

With soilless composts the NPK ratio is often 15:8:10. Constant watering of the plants will slowly leach out the macronutrients, especially the potassium, and after about four weeks it is advisable to commence liquid feeding. By this time it will probably have become necessary to water the soilless composts every other day (or even daily with the smaller pots) and, under these circumstances, the 'inorganic nutrients' would be rapidly washed out of the compost. A balanced liquid feed of NPK 15:15:15 diluted to one-quarter strength is given at every other watering. The compost should be thoroughly wetted and the excess liquid allowed to drain away freely. For the final six weeks before flowering it would be wise to change the formulation to NPK 15:15:20, but note that this is not a drastic change, merely increasing the potassium levels while maintaining an adequate supply of nitrogen and phosphorous. A massive change in the potassium levels could alter the whole character of the plant making it woody rather than succulent. Auxiliary feeding should be continued even as the blooms are developing. The possibility of high potassium feeds causing a magnesium deficiency has already been remarked upon and it is suggested that magnesium sulphate (Epsom salts) should also be applied at two-week intervals once the change to the 15:15:20 fertiliser has been made — 1 teaspoon (5g) to 1 gallon of water is recommended. An alternative approach is to anticipate the need for magnesium and to use Dolomite limestone (which contains magnesium carbonate) as a part replacement for ground chalk in the mixing of the compost.

If loam-based composts are being used then they will not dry out at anything like the same rate as the peat type. Watering these composts can, therefore, be a less frequent operation and it is suggested that liquid feeds should be applied once each week but at half the recommended strength. Excellent liquid feeds covering a range of NPK ratios are widely available at garden centres and the usual horticultural outlets but for those who wish to mix their own the following formulations may be tried. For loam-based composts the John Innes Liquid feed is quite satisfactory and easily prepared from the following ingredients:

15oz (425g) ammonium sulphate
$2\frac{3}{4}$oz (78g) potassium nitrate
$2\frac{1}{4}$oz (64g) monoammonium phosphate

The recommended strength of this solution is 1oz (28g) per gallon of water thus providing an NPK value of 18:6:6.

Another mix which has been used successfully as a bloom feed is:

$\frac{1}{2}$oz (14g) potassium nitrate
$\frac{1}{2}$oz (14g) potassium phosphate

These quantities are dissolved in two gallons of water. This is a high potash feed with an NPK ratio of 6:25:40. With this feed magnesium deficiency could be a problem.

For soilless composts the following formulation should prove satisfactory:

$\frac{1}{4}$oz (7g) Urea
$\frac{1}{2}$oz (14g) potassium nitrate
$\frac{1}{2}$oz (14g) potassium phosphate

These quantities should be dissolved in two gallons of water.

Though not classed as a feed in the ordinary sense, an application of sequestered iron (together with other trace elements) given twice at an eight-day interval will help considerably in maintaining the rich colouring of the blooms.

Finally it must be pointed out that the acidity or alkalinity of the compost can greatly affect the availability of the various elements to the plants. The acidity is usually measured and expressed as the pH of the medium — this is a scale which normally ranges from 1 to 14 — acid media have low numbers, alkaline ones have high numbers and the pH of neutral water is 7. The best pH for begonia cultivation is 6.5 to 6.8 and most peats are more acidic than this. Many of the large chemists will sell special pH indicator papers which, when pressed against the moist medium, will register the pH by a colour change. Any tendency for the compost to become too acidic may be corrected by an occasional watering with dilute lime water.

Though undoubtedly these auxiliary liquid feeds have a part to play in the successful cultivation of begonias they should always be looked upon as merely adding icing to the cake; good cultivation and consistency will lay the foundations for good flowers and plants.

Staking

One week after final potting a stake for each main stem should be inserted into the compost and at about 2in distance from the base of the stem. In the early stages of growth the stems may

Figure 3.11 Staked Plant — All Growth Facing Forward

only measure some $\frac{1}{2}$in in diameter, but ultimately they should develop into $1\frac{1}{2}$in trunks and support will become essential. Bamboo canes of at least $\frac{5}{8}$in diameter or $\frac{5}{8}$in square wooden stakes make ideal supports — for the large plants they need to be at least 3ft long. When inserting the stake great care should be taken not to impale the tuber. The stake should be set at a slight angle so that the centre of the plant is opened up to allow good air circulation. The stem is tied loosely to the stake using good quality broad raffia or the newer polypropylene ties. The tie should be made just above a leaf axil. As growth continues and the stems expand, a careful watch should be maintained to avoid stem damage.

Unsupported stems of a well grown begonia can be easily snapped off either at a node or at the base of the stem. Mature plants should not be moved unless they have been staked.

It is considered unsightly to have stakes protruding above the foliage of fully grown plants.

Humidity

Tuberous begonias thrive in a humid atmosphere but this must be accompanied by warmth. At the beginning of the season (early spring — March/April in Britain) and at the end of the season (autumn — September/October in Britain) humidity is not a problem, but warmth is. At the height of the summer (June/August in Britain) warmth is no problem, but humidity certainly is.

By far the best method of maintaining a reasonable level of humidity (60-70 per cent) is by the use of misting nozzles placed below bench height and used very frequently during hot weather. Even when used overhead they will do very little damage to any but the largest buds as long as the 0.02in-0.03in nozzles are used. In the absence of misting nozzles then under-bench flooding may be employed, but this is only effective when a polythene liner has been laid below the gravel.

Humidification should be discontinued around mid-afternoon so that some drying out can take place before the inevitable temperature drop occurs in the early evening. High humidity accompanied by low temperatures provides the ideal environment for the onset of powdery mildew.

Ventilation

As has already been indicated, begonias develop much better

and remain much healthier when adequate ventilation is available and when good air circulation is encouraged. Once the danger of really cold evenings has passed then top and bottom ventilation must be available 24 hours per day. On really hot days some means of forced ventilation, e.g. a 12in extractor fan, can be beneficial since with small greenhouses the internal temperatures can rise rapidly into the low hundreds (100-120°F). Of course good air circulation will not be achieved if adequate space is not given to each plant on the bench. Overcrowding of plants can result in their becoming 'leggy'. Towards the end of the season when temperatures are low and humidity high this overcrowding can lead to widespread attacks of stem rot and the possible loss of plants.

Stopping

Plants being grown for exhibition or competition must be encouraged to produce the largest flowers possible without resorting to coarse or distorted blooms and die back. To this end plants are stopped by pinching out the growing tips at the correct time; this will be further discussed on page 86. Plants must be stopped, however, for reasons other than showing. Left to themselves, begonias in the greenhouse will continue to flower, the blooms becoming smaller as the season continues. The tubers would have only a very short dormant period before being started up again the following year. Pinching out the growing tips in mid-September (early autumn) will prevent any further flowers from being produced and the plant will be slowly forced into dormancy. After this stopping the quantity of water

Figure 3.12
Tuberous Begonias
— Stems Reduced at
the End of the
Season

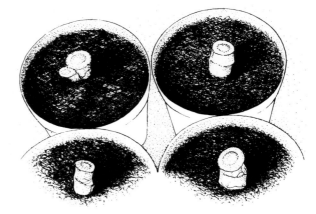

60

being given should be gradually reduced and a pinch of sulphate of potash given on a single occasion — this will help to harden the tubers. Water must not be entirely withheld at this stage since it is now that the tuber should undergo an increase in size. This increase in tuber size appears to take place when the daily and night temperatures fall to about 45°F (7°C). By late autumn the leaves will have yellowed and many will have fallen from the plants; greenhouse hygiene is now of the essence and dead leaves must be continually cleared away from plants and benches. When all the leaves have fallen, the main stems can be cut down to within 3-4in of the tuber. Stacking the pots on their sides will allow the remainder of the stems to fall away without remaining on the surface of the compost where they could set up rots.

Plants in Flower

Blooms of the large-flowered tuberous double begonias are very susceptible to becoming marked when touched. This is particularly the case with the scarlet and crimson-flowered cultivars where the merest touching by hand, clothing or begonia foliage will almost certainly leave brown marks which will only develop some time after the event. It is often sensible to turn those plants which are adjacent to the pathway so that their blooms face towards the greenhouse walls. Fully open blooms do not like a high humidity and though all colours will suffer it is the red shades which fare the worst, the edges of the flowers turning brown. White blooms frequently develop brown or black spots. This problem is solved by simply reducing atmospheric humidity and watering the plants before mid-afternoon.

Though many modern cultivars have been bred to have stiff flower stems, nevertheless a well grown flower head will often tend to 'look down' to the bench rather than look at you eye to eye. Anticipating this, therefore, a sensible precaution is to place an extending bloom support so that the stirrup is just supporting the neck of the bloom. As the bloom develops so the support is extended to keep the head of flower in the correct forward-looking position. If placed under the large buds early enough, the supports may be used judiciously to move the blooms slightly laterally for better overall effect, e.g. a bloom which faces inwards may be persuaded to take up a better position.

Any leaves which prevent the proper opening of the flower

should be gently moved out of the way or even, as a very last resort, removed from the plant.

At this stage of the growth cycle an insect infestation or a fungal attack can be a great problem since insecticides or fungicides may not be applied as sprays. The only course of action is to use smoke generators; these also must be handled carefully since they usually require the greenhouse to be completely closed. This is a time when compromise is the sensible approach. Eventually, perhaps after two weeks or so, some of the early blooms will begin to die — these should be removed immediately. Dying flowers frequently release ethylene into the atmosphere and this can cause the premature demise of the flowers which are following on. Flowering time has been a long time coming so that it is well worthwhile taking that extra amount of care and attention to maintain the flowers at the peak of perfection for as long as possible.

Tuber Harvesting and Storage

The tubers may be removed from the compost when all stems have gone or, if necessary, they remain in the pots. When removed from the pots all compost and the dead roots are brushed away and the tuber examined for rot or vine weevil infestation. Any rot is cut away with a sharp knife and the wound dusted with othocide/green sulphur. If there is any sign of vine weevil then the grubs or larvae must be dug out immediately and suitable insecticides incorporated into the compost next year. The tubers should now be stored, correctly labelled, in very slightly moist peat and in a frost free but cool (40°F) place. Begonia tubers really need to have up to an eight-week period of dormancy before being started again into growth.

Cascade or Pendula Begonias

The cultivation of pendula begonias parallels exactly that described for the large-flowered doubles except that they do require as long a growing season as possible. They need to be started as early in the year as is feasible. On being removed from the propagator they are potted into 3in pots where they will remain for four to six weeks. During this period they need to be kept in a fairly warm environment, certainly no less than 55°F (12.8°C), to ensure an adequate growth rate. When the roots are beginning to run around the sides of the pot the plants are removed to a suitable hanging basket. A 12in diameter wire or plastic basket can accommodate up to three plants (from small one to two-year-old tubers) or one plant (from an older, larger tuber).

The basket is first lined, preferably with sphagnum moss; this not only looks attractive but is excellent for moisture retention. A number of synthetic liners are also currently on the market which, while probably very good for the retention of water, certainly add nothing to the attractiveness of the basket. The lining is carried out so that the moss extends to perhaps 1in above the rim of the basket. Having lined the container, a layer of fibrous loam, containing a small amount of admixed bone meal, is then added so that it reaches about halfway up the basket. Having decided on how many tubers are to be grown, an empty pot of the same size is positioned in the basket for each tuber. Compost identical to that being used for the large-flowered types is now used to fill the spaces around the empty pots. The empty pots are removed carefully and replaced by the growing plants and the compost gently firmed with the fingers. It is important that the 1in lip at the top of the basket liner is maintained in order to assist in watering later on.

The finished basket can stand on top of an 8in pot on the greenhouse bench to be hung up only when the trailing stems reach bench level.

The basket must be kept well watered (not waterlogged) and would benefit from dipping into a large bucket of water once every two weeks. All flower buds are removed until the plants are well established and the trailing stems are at least 12in long. Feeding with a liquid 15:15:30 fertiliser at this stage would be beneficial. It must be remembered that, unlike the large-flowered doubles, the female flowers are always left on the pendula begonias to enhance the beauty of the plant. Towards the end of the season the plants are stopped by pinching out the growing tips and dormancy encouraged in the normal way.

It is the usual practice to use only one cultivar to each basket. Apart from the fact that different cultivars have slightly different growth habits it is difficult to see why this practice has developed.

Tuberous Begonias in the Garden

A number of tuberous begonias, e.g. Multiflora, Fimbriata, Marginata, Non-Stops and the large-flowered doubles may be grown quite successfully and flowered out of doors. The plants used in this way may be either those reared as seedlings (described on page 37) or they may have been grown from tubers started in the greenhouse and in their first pots (described on page 49).

The site chosen should be selected with some care and prepared well in advance. The most ideal position is one which is protected from the hot midday sun and from strong winds. Even when correctly and carefully hardened off, tuberous begonia blooms and foliage can easily scorch.

The bed should be well dug and enriched with humus; peat, spent hops, compost etc. worked well into the soil will help to keep the medium moist and ideal for begonia cultivation. Any balanced fertiliser added to the top 3in and applied at the rate of 1oz (28g) to 3 sq.yds will be beneficial. Tuberous begonias are relatively shallow rooting plants and the roots tend to grow horizontally. If the garden soil is of a heavy type it helps considerably to place a layer of sand about 6in below the soil surface, thus assisting good drainage.

If it is not possible to select a position shaded from the midday sun then a shade cloth awning some 4-5ft above the plants should be arranged.

The young plants (seedlings or tubers) should be planted out spaced at 9-12in intervals and arranged so that the tips of the leaves are facing outwards. Any flower buds which appear during the next four or five weeks should be removed, thus helping the plant to become properly established. Seedling plants or tubers which were started in the greenhouse should be planted out in early June (early summer) after being hardened off in a cold frame from late May (late spring). Tubers can, however, be planted directly into the beds at 2-2½in deep in May (late spring). By the time the shoots have appeared above the surface all danger of frost should have gone. Tubers planted directly into the ground will produce plants with a shorter flowering season than those started in the greenhouse, but during the summer the beds should be a mass of colour. Female flower buds are not removed from begonias grown out of doors and, since these plants do not usually grow very tall, staking is rarely needed. Flower heads should be removed as soon as they show signs of browning and the beds should be kept nicely moist at all times.

Begonias can be safely left in the garden until late autumn — they will not suffer from one or two light frosts, but a succession of two or three hard frosts will do incalcuable damage, completely ruining the tuber. In late September (early autumn) the growing tips are taken out and some four weeks later the stems are cut down to about 6in. Adequate protection from a light frost may be obtained by laying lightweight polythene over the plants each evening and removing it the following morning.

These few weeks of low temperatures are important in the cultivation of begonias since it is the time when tubers increase in size. In certain parts of the USA the fall or autumn is so brief that seedlings have insufficient time to form tubers so they are raised simply as annual plants.

A few days after being cut down, the tubers are lifted with a ball of soil and stored in trays in a cool, airy and frost-free shed or outbuilding. The remaining pieces of stem will fall away within three weeks, at which time all the soil should be brushed away from the tuber. Begonias grown from seed do need a longer growing season than many other bedding plants; for those with unheated greenhouses this means delaying seed sowing until April (mid-spring). Growers confronted with this problem might find it advantageous to purchase seedling plants from a recognised specialist begonia nursery.

In certain parts of the country vine weevil can be a great problem and if its presence is suspected then precautions should be taken when the bedding site is being prepared. Carbaryl (Sevin) incorporated into the soil around each plant will help to keep this pest at bay.

The period during which the seedling plants are in full flower is the time to grade them with a view to future cultivation. This is particularly the case with one's own experimental crosses though it should apply equally to seedlings raised from purchased seed. The whole process of assessing plant and bloom quality is one which should help to develop in the grower a critical eye for what is good. Of course it is difficult to assess

Figure 3.13
Tuberous Double
Begonia, Unnamed
Seedling

colour quality properly on plants grown in the open since many of the paler colours are considerably changed when cultivated under the protection of glass. However, certain characteristics can be dealt with quite ruthlessly, e.g. any plants with single or semi-double flowers should be discarded together with any that have spindly growth or badly shaped blooms. Plants to be selected for further cultivation should be of sturdy habit with a pronounced tendency to produce side-shoots and they should have stiff flower stems which bear flowers of a nice rounded shape with symmetrically arranged petals. Flowers with very few petals should not be considered worthwhile but then neither should those which possess a multitude of small petals. The balance to be sought comes only with experience but some guidance can be found by studying other named cultivars. Any plant with what appears to be a new colour break should be kept for further cultivation.

Plants having all these attributes will be rare indeed, but any one with some of these characteristics will be well worth marking as a potential greenhouse subject for the following year. Indeed it is worth considering devising your own points system on which to assess a plant's performance in its first year. A suggested approach to pointing could be:

Plant Habit (20)	Sturdiness/vigour	10
	Side-shoots	5
	Erect and Sturdy Flower Stems	5
Flower Quality (20)	Colour	5
	Roundness	5
	Flower Depth	5
	Petal Quality	5

These points should be considered as maxima to be awarded for the perfect plant or flower and marks should be deducted for anything less than the best. For example, a mark of 5 should be given for colour only when there is no cultivar known to you of the same colour. As a general rule the depth of a begonia bloom should be about half the diameter and anything less than that should incur a penalty. Though flower size at this stage is not necessarily a high priority, nevertheless plants with flowers less than about 5-6in in diameter are not likely to justify further cultivation unless they have some other extenuating feature. A total score of 28-30 marks should justify that seedling being grown on next year under more protective conditions.

This type of record or assessment, together with the plant

identification, will assist in following any change in characteristics which might occur during the subsequent years. Undoubtedly the novice grower will tend to be over generous with the points allocation in the early years, but will become more critical as familiarity with begonias increases. This approach is all part of educating oneself in the critical appraisal of begonias.

While the cultivation of tuberous begonias has been discussed in great detail it is not the intention in this book to consider the growing of the non-tuberous types in anything more than a superficial way. Sufficient detail will, however, be presented so that the plants will grow reasonably well and the reader's interest in this type of begonia will be stimulated.

Non-Tuberous Begonias

Hiemalis and Cheimantha Types

In Britain, the Hiemalis and Cheimantha type begonias are purchased as rooted offshoots of the parent plants. As we have already noted, most of these begonias do not have female flowers and therefore set no seed. Though one or two Lorraine begonias (Cheimantha type) are still available, their use as

Figure 3.14 Double-flowered Rieger Begonia

winter flowering plants has been largely superseded by the Hiemalis group and more particularly, the Rieger begonias. In Europe, Rieger begonias are among the most popular and sought-after houseplants. Cultivation of the two groups is very similar except that the Cheimantha begonias are slightly more tolerant of low temperatures. For the best results it is necessary to maintain a minimum temperature of 55°F (12.8°C) throughout the entire year. They will grow well in an open compost and the following mix is suggested:

> 2 parts by volume fibrous loam
> 1 part by volume leaf mould
> 1 part by volume sphagnum peat
> 1 part by volume $\frac{1}{8}$in grit

To this compost should be added the recommended amount of a proprietary base fertiliser.

Usually these begonias are bought as young plants in 4-5in pots from mid-spring to mid-summer and, on receiving them they should be repotted into the 6-7in size. The compost needs only to be settled by gentle firming — these plants do not like to be hard potted.

After repotting they should be grown on in a well lit position but not in direct sunlight. If they are being grown on a window ledge then the pot should be turned a little each day to ensure uniform growth and flowering. They are very susceptible to root rot and should not, therefore, be overwatered. Water need only be given when the plant is beginning to dry out and it should be kept off the foliage. When watering, the compost should be thoroughly wetted and the excess be allowed to drain away freely. Within a few weeks of being repotted the plant should have developed a good root system and feeding can begin. Any reliable liquid feed with an NPK value of 20:20:20 will prove suitable and it should be applied at only half the recommended strength and at three-week intervals. These begonias cannot be classed as heavy feeders and too much fertiliser will assuredly lead to a lot of leaf growth at the expense of flowers. This will be even more marked if the light levels are low. It is advisable to remove any flower buds until the repotted plant has recovered from its transplant shock. In a few establishments it has become the practice to repot in a slightly different way to overcome this partial setback to growth. The existing pot is cut with a sharp knife so that fairly large sections can be removed without disturbing the plant; the plant (with its pot) is then dropped on into the next size together with the necessary compost.

Figure 3.15 Staking
Rieger Begonias

Figure 3.16 Rieger
Begonias in a
Commercial
Nursery

This type of begonia will continue to produce masses of flowers right through the summer and into the late autumn. For the best flowering results they do prefer a uniform temperature of 60-65°F (15.5-18°C), good light and plenty of air circulation — atmospheric humidity is not critical. As the plants increase in size it may be necessary to provide a little support in the form of stakes. These should be thin canes placed around the sides of the pot so that their presence is unobtrusive. One or two of the modern cultivars have rather tall-growing slender stems and these should lend themselves to basket cultivation.

As the winter approaches plants grown in the house should be moved to a southerly aspect to increase the amount of light and thus encourage winter flowering. It has been suggested that further encouragement to flower in winter might be achieved by subjecting the plants to twelve hours' complete darkness each day for four weeks.

The winter-flowering begonias appear to suffer from two major problems; one is a susceptibility to powdery mildew and the other is the attentions of white fly. Good air circulation and a warm environment will help to reduce the likelihood of a mildew attack, but if one does occur then a spray with Dinocap (Karathane) (Doo Spray) must be given. White fly needs to be treated with resmethrin and the treatment repeated every ten days for three or four weeks. After the heavy flowering of autumn and winter the amount of water given should be gradually reduced in February (late winter) and the temperature may be lowered to 55°F (12.8°C). New growths will appear in April/May (mid-late spring), at which time the old growths should be cut back to about 2-3in. The plant should be knocked out of its pot, much of the old root ball shaken off and then it should be repotted into a smaller size pot. Bottom heat of around 60°F (15.5°C) will now encourage a good start to the new season.

It must be said that many people do find it very difficult to bring these winter-flowering begonias safely through the resting period but usually this is due to keeping the compost too damp or having too low a temperature or, more likely, a combination of both. It is, therefore, very necessary to propagate the plants to guard against the possible loss of the parents. Propagation must be by either leaf or stem cuttings and, though leaf cuttings will give more basal shoots, most growers use stem cuttings.

The new basal growths undoubtedly make the best cuttings and, taken off when they are a few inches high, they will root quickly in an open peat-sand medium with a bottom heat of 65°F (18°C). Stem cuttings taken during the flowering season and especially those from stems which have already flowered may also be rooted but they rarely make good plants.

Semperflorens Begonias

In Britain and Europe by far the greatest use made of semps is as bedding or mass outdoor display plants. In relation to the overall plant size the large proportion of bloom makes this group of begonias highly suited to this application. Many of these single-flowered cultivars are F1 hybrids noted for their vigour. All are grown from seed sown in heat in January (late winter) and, after hardening off, it is safe to plant these seedlings in early June (early summer) into beds already well prepared and rich in humus. As a group the semps will not thrive in heavy, wet soil so a well drained site is essential. Though they can happily withstand high light levels they will not tolerate long exposure to intense midday sunlight. While dense, shady positions should be avoided, it is possible to afford some protection by planting fairly close to other taller plants. Cultivars which have bronze-coloured foliage appear to be less susceptible to scorch than those with light-green leaves, though the difference is not great. Most of the cultivars employed as bedding plants do have a natural tendency to become bushy, but this can be considerably helped by pinching out the growing tips when the plants are about 4in high. Though, as has been said, semps do not like wet growing conditions, neither do they appreciate arid dryness. In periods of hot weather, therefore, it is wise to spray them overhead regularly.

When grown at their best most modern cultivars are extremely free flowering and this means considerable quantities of decaying vegetable matter around the plants. With careful attention to cultivation and plant hygiene the semps will provide a continuous display of colour right up to the onset of frost.

It is the normal practice to treat these bedding subjects strictly as annuals sowing new seed each year. One can, however, pot up and grow on individual plants for either greenhouse or home decoration. This can be very rewarding especially with some of the latest double-flowered or variegated foliage cultivars. These are rarely grown from seed being usually purchased as young plants propagated from cuttings. They make particularly attractive subjects for indoor gardens and patio displays.

The dislike shown by semps for excessive moisture at the

roots means that a very open compost is required for successful pot cultivation. A simple but adequate growing mix would be:

1 part by volume fibrous loam
^{1}2 part by volume sphagnum peat
^{1}2 part by volume ^{1}sin grit

Alternatively, one of the commercially available soilless composts may be used, though 1 part by volume grit to 4 parts by volume of the compost should be added to it. The use of clay pots is to be encouraged since they dry out quickly and aeration of the root system is assisted. Most cultivars in this group appear to respond much better when the pot is quickly filled with root, so overpotting is to be discouraged. The Calla Lily cultivars, however, do prefer a somewhat larger pot size than the other semps.

Semps will thrive in an abundance of light but not direct sunlight and, conversely, low light levels will result in spindly growth. A growing temperature of 60-65°F (15.5-18°C) is ideal. This, together with their undemanding humidity requirements, makes them very rewarding houseplants. Regular feeding with a good balanced fertiliser applied at half strength every two weeks during the growing season will help to maintain vigorous, healthy growth. As with the bedding subjects, pinching out the growth points will produce sturdy, bushy plants. Apart from the possibility of root rot from overwatering, the main threat to semps is powdery mildew. At the first sign of infection the whole plant must be sprayed with Dinocap. The growth rate of semps slows down during the shorter daylight months, but gradually the plants will increase in size and require potting on. They should be moved in the spring using the next pot size only.

Propagation of semps is by cuttings, but this is not always easy — many losses occur. It is far better to simply divide the plants in the spring and grow each part on in the normal way.

Cane-stemmed Begonias

An editor of *The Begonian* once described cane-stemmed begonias as 'Almost as American as mom and apple pie — nearly every rural grandmother had — indeed has — an angel-wing begonia.' While that may indeed be the case, this type of begonia, or at least the more recent cultivars, have not had quite the same impact here in Europe. Quite a lot of people grow B. Lucerna, it is true, and quite a large selection of the species are to be found, but the great strides forward which have been made in this group have been due to the Americans and, perhaps to a lesser extent, the Japanese. This situation is unfortunate since many of the recent hybrids are very beautiful and highly decorative plants which grow remarkably well in the home as well as the greenhouse.

The majority of the cane-stemmed begonias are fairly tall growers, i.e. 1-6ft tall, and this should be remembered when selecting a suitable spot to grow them. To produce good foliage and flowers they require plenty of light, in fact as much sunlight as they can stand without scorching the foliage. It is the general experience that cane-stemmed begonias respond better than most to a heavier compost and to a regular feeding programme. A suitable growing medium for these begonias can be made from the following ingredients:

2 parts by volume sphagnum peat
1 part by volume leaf mould
1 part by volume fibrous loam
1 part by volume composted farmyard manure
1 part by volume sharp grit

To each 8 gallons of this mix should be added:

3oz (85g) ground limestone
3$\frac{1}{2}$oz (98g) bone meal

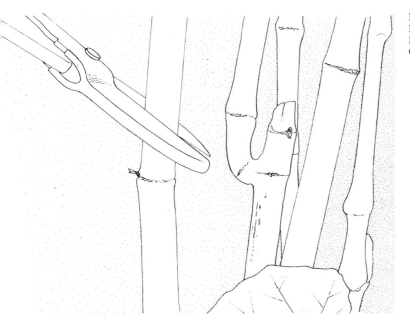

Figure 3.17 Annual Pruning of Begonia Lucerna — Note Outward-facing Bud

$\frac{1}{2}$oz (14g) dried blood
4oz (115g) superphosphate of lime
$2\frac{1}{4}$oz (64g) sulphate of potash

Plants are potted into the above compost in the spring — a young, freshly rooted cutting needs a 4in pot and more mature plants, larger containers. Cane-stemmed begonias require a temperature of 58-70°F (14.4-21°C) and watering only when they show obvious signs of beginning to dry out. Overwatering will result in the loss of the lower leaves. As the young plants grow it is advisable to pinch out the growing tip and this should be done at the stage when the lower leaves have fully developed. This pinching out will encourage basal growth. Regular feeding with a 20:20:20 liquid fertiliser in the growing season is necessary for the development of the maximum amount of bloom. With mature plants regular pruning has to be carried out, partly to maintain plant vigour but also to improve plant shape. The older canes should be cut back in early spring to 3-5 nodes above the compost surface, graduating the heights of the pruned canes. The cut should be made at about $\frac{3}{4}$-1in above a node, the bud of which is facing outwards, thus indicating the direction in which it will grow. To avoid the risk of infecting the plant during pruning it is advisable to dip the pruning knife or shears in methylated spirit. The cut surface should be dusted with a mixture of green sulphur and orthocide.

Figure 3.18 Pruning
Completed

If, after repeated pruning, the plant becomes 'hollow centred' then a few canes may be cut to an inward facing node or nodal bud.

Cane-stemmed begonias have two major enemies: one is root knot eelworm and the other is mealybug. Any infestation by nematodes has almost certainly been introduced in the loam used in the compost, and a sensible precaution would be to sterilise it before use. Evidence of possible nematode attack is a gradual swelling of the roots, yellowing of the leaves and the ultimate death of the plant, often during the autumn. All containers to be used with the cane-stemmed begonias should be thoroughly sterilised before use.

Mealybug can be dealt with by wiping the 'cotton-wool' infection with a pad soaked in methylated spirit and watering a solution of malathion into the compost.

Propagation of cane-stemmed begonias is simplicity itself. Stem tip cuttings are removed with about three nodes and are then placed in clean water with one node below the surface. Within 14 days small roots will begin to form and, when they are $\frac{1}{2}$in long, they are potted up and grown on.

Cane-stemmed begonias may also be grown from seed but the seedlings only come true when the species are selfed.

Shrub-like Begonias

This group of begonias may be cultivated in the same general way as the cane-stemmed types; they require a similar temperature range of around 62-65°F (17-18°C), good light levels but not direct sunlight, and are not demanding on atmospheric humidity (40-60 per cent). They may be grown successfully in the compost described for the cane-stemmed begonias but will do well enough in a well drained, open soilless medium. Plant management requires that growing tips should be pinched out to encourage bushy growth, and periodic pruning of the older stems to improve plant symmetry. In the spring when new growth commences, regular feeding with a balanced fertiliser is carried out, though increased phosphorous and potassium levels are employed just before the flowering period, i.e. a 13:25:25 composition. Propagation of the shrub-like begonias is by stem cuttings rooted in water.

Figure 3.19 Rooting
Cutting in Water

Figure 3.20 Cutting
After Being Rooted
in Water

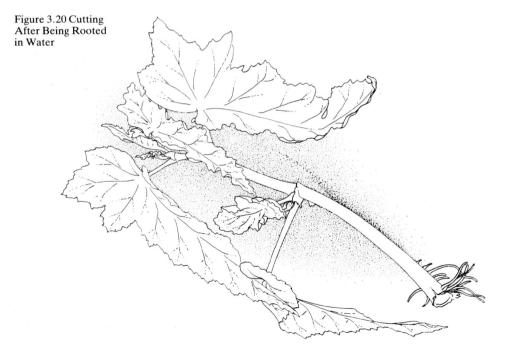

Rex Begonias and Rhizomatous Types

The majority of Rex begonias are rhizomatous though a few which have tuberous begonias in their background are not entirely so. Though the cultivation of Rex and the rhizomatous group have some differences, they have enough in common to be treated here together.

Like many other begonias these types do not like to be exposed to full sun. Of the two groups the rhizomatous begonias will prefer the higher light levels — excessive light will cause the foliage to lose its colour and too little light will cause the leaf stalks to become elongated. Rhizomatous begonias prefer a temperature range of 60-65°F (15.6-18°C) while the Rex type do better at 65-70°F (18-21°C). In winter when light levels are low, both groups tend to become dormant during which time the plants need to be kept fairly dry at the roots. In the case of mature plants this dormancy may be encouraged by slightly lowering the temperatures in late December (mid-winter); young plants, however, should be kept growing through the winter.

Atmospheric humidity is beneficial to these foliage begonias and it helps to keep the leaves in good condition. A relative humidity of 60 per cent is a satisfactory level to aim for. Too low a humidity will often result in a curling of the leaves and, in the

Figure 3.21 Begonia Rex 'Merry Christmas'

case of the Rexes, browning of the leaf margins. Considerable care must be taken, however, to ensure that high humidity is accompanied by warm conditions and good air circulation to avoid attacks of powdery mildew. The species *B. masoniana* ('Iron Cross') is particularly susceptible to fungal infection. Both groups of plants are shallow rooting and are best grown in pans or half pots using a growing medium containing leaf mould. A suitable compost for these begonias is:

> 1 part by volume sieved leaf mould
> 1 part by volume fibrous loam
> 1 part by volume silver sand

When the plants come out of their dormancy and are growing well in the spring, a regular application of a balanced fertiliser every third week will greatly assist in maintaining a healthy plant.

Watering must be done carefully and only when the compost is just becoming dry. Since wetting the foliage can readily cause rot, it is addvisable to stand the pan in a container of water rather than to water overhead. A continuously wet compost will certainly lead to rhizome rotting. Both types of begonia seem to prefer to be slightly rootbound. Plant management includes pinching out the rhizome tips when they reach the sides of the pan and this encourages branching and a better shaped plant.

During dormancy, and particularly when the temperature falls too low, the Rex begonias may lose their foliage. With the coming of spring, however, new growth will begin again as long as the rhizome is intact.

Propagation of both groups is usually by leaf sections or by rhizome sections.

CHAPTER 4

Begonias for Showing and Exhibiting

While the personal challenge of growing and flowering good plants is sufficient for the majority of amateurs, the numerous competitive flower shows around the country are evidence enough that, for some, a greater challenge is called for.

One sight which can be breathtaking in its beauty is a group display of begonias. Such displays, in some instances requiring a maximum of twenty pots but in others unrestricted, are seen in a number of the summer shows in Britain, and in some cases these too might be competitive.

There is little doubt that the competitive spirit can be all-consuming, and we must all be aware of instances when the desire to win replaces a genuine love for the beauty of the flower. It is sad to meet someone for whom a new cultivar is merely another potential show winner. However, in the following pages we shall attempt to set down guidelines which, though intended for the competitor will also encourage the amateur to strive for the best. In the main that which follows is largely related to the showing of tuberous double begonias.

General Cultivation

The methods of growing begonias for exhibition are in general identical to those already described in detail for greenhouse display. The composts used are the same, feeding programmes are similar etc. — it is the attention to detail which ultimately matters and which will make a good plant into a show plant.

For the majority of the middle and late shows in Britain (August-September) tubers should be started between late February and March. There is much to be gained from choosing named cultivars for competition — their flowering and growth habits and their potential are well known to the judges. Unnamed cultivars may of course be used, but they must have a quality which is known by the grower to be good, e.g. the plant habit should be well branched and the flowers of good shape. Many exhibitors take a rather casual and cavalier attitude at the beginning of the season though the serious competitor is already planning his or her strategy long before the tubers are started into growth.

Show Schedule

Either the current year's or the previous year's schedule should be consulted so that the general feel of the classes may be obtained. Are the classes divided into novices, intermediates, senior and open classes; are there classes for cut blooms and/or pot plants; what about group classes or maybe hanging baskets; are there restrictions on pot sizes; is there a minimum or maximum number of cultivars which may be used in any one class; are we familiar with the accepted colour classification of all our cultivars? These points, and many others can be sorted out by a careful scrutiny of the schedule even before the season begins, and a rough plan of campaign may be drawn up.

Cut Blooms or Pot Plants or Group Display

Cut bloom classes, as the name suggests, are those in which only the flower heads are displayed, either singly (usually only for novice growers) or in groups of three, six or twelve. The flowers are displayed on boards, and it is well to find out whether the organisers provide these or not. The best cut blooms are grown on single-stemmed plants and preferably on two or three-year-old tubers.

Pot plants intended for group display are usually grown from slightly more mature tubers, say three or four years old, and are frequently cultivated as a single stem with two substantial side-shoots. Plants to be shown in pot plant classes, whether as single specimens or as multiple pots should be multi-stemmed, i.e. at least three main stems each carrying side-shoots. It follows, therefore, that a decision has to be made very early in the season as to what is intended for each and every plant. Any cultivar intended to produce cut blooms must have all growths in excess of one removed and used as cuttings. Any plant to be used in a group display should have excess growths removed leaving the two strongest to be flowered. With the pot plant classes the plant chosen to compete as a single specimen should have at least three stems growing in such directions as to produce flowers all round the pot. Plants designed for the multi-pot classes should have at least two stems from which the ultimate flowers will cover about 120° of arc when viewed from the front.

It should be quite unnecessary to use a pot size greater than 7in diameter, and there are many successful growers who would go no larger than 6in. No side-shoots are allowed to develop and this does not necessarily mean using them as cuttings, but rather removing them before they develop. As with all begonias they must be grown very cool and with as much ventilation as can be provided and as much light as they can accept without scorching. The plants should have plenty of air space around them and be arranged in groups of identical cultivars. Once in their final pots and securely staked, feeding should be commenced about four weeks later and when the pots contain plenty of root. Any liquid feed of NPK 15:15:30 with trace elements will benefit the plants and flowers. A number of cut bloom growers like to alternate the liquid feed between the organic nutrient type and the inorganic variety. Once again feeding is at every other watering and at one-quarter recommended strength.

All flower buds should be removed up to about eight weeks before the show. At four weeks before the show date remove any buds which measure more than $2\frac{1}{2}$in across the widest place. At this stage there should be two well developed buds visible, one which is about $1\frac{1}{2}$in in size and a second bud somewhat smaller in size. The larger of the two will be the one which will ultimately produce the cut bloom and, like all other male flowers, will be flanked by two smaller buds. At the same time as securing the flower bud the growing tip of the plant should be removed. After a further week the smaller bud is removed and from now on the whole energy of the plant is channelled into the growth of the one remaining male flower bud. The two flanking buds are removed as soon as they are big enough for the operation to be carried out without damaging or even touching the central bud. The major objective now is to try to keep the growing conditions as constant as possible, avoiding wide fluctuations in temperature or humidity. Adequate ventilation must be given and the greenhouse must be kept as cool as possible. The development of this bud to fully opened flower will depend not only on the light and heat conditions but also on the cultivar, e.g. the named begonia 'Red Admiral' will be at its best up to two weeks earlier than, say, the cultivar 'Roy Hartley'. It is indeed partly the idiosyncratic behaviour of different cultivars which ultimately transforms the cultivation of begonias from a science to an art. It is advisable to grow more than one plant of each cultivar in an attempt to 'bracket' the show date and thus improve the chances of having perfect blooms 'on the day'. It is also

Cut Blooms

important to remember that blooms continue to grow even when they are apparently fully open so that the feeding regime should be continued right up to the show date. One of the avowed objectives of the present day hybridiser is to produce new cultivars which have strong, erect flower stems; alas this is not always achieved. It is very necessary to use adjustable supports placed under the neck of the flower to maintain it in the correct forward-looking position. As the flower increases in size there is some danger that the lower dorsal petal may touch the wire support. A small wodge of cotton wool inserted between the wire and the petal will prevent damage to the flower. Any leaf which is touching the developing bud should be gently moved out of the way since, if the bloom is to develop uniformly, nothing must inhibit the growth. Any leaf which cannot be moved out of the way must be removed from the plant.

As the show bud begins to open, i.e. it is 'oyster like', the greenhouse humidity should be reduced to about 40 per cent, no watering of the plants should take place after midday, and full ventilation must be maintained.

With most modern cultivars there is no great difficulty in achieving 7in diameter blooms, but the extra one or two inches will require that extra careful cultivation. Heavy feeding will most probably produce multi-centred or distorted blooms or a breakdown in pigmentation. High temperatures with excessive sunlight can also result in colour blotching or colour 'running' in picotees. Continuous caring for the plants to ensure absolute consistency of cultivation is most likely to produce that extra size and perfection.

Cutting and Transporting

If the blooms are going to be staged at their best it is essential that they are cut at the latest possible time. The plants should have been watered some hours earlier and the flowers cut with a sharp knife, keeping the flower stems as long as possible. The end of the flower stem is wrapped in damp cotton wool or alternatively a small rubber balloon containing water is slipped over the stem. Holding the bloom by the neck of the stem it is carefully placed in a suitable container. The deep flower boxes used by florists are ideal receptacles and they should be lined with a 1in deep layer of cotton wool. A number of horseshoe collars of cotton wool or tissue are then placed in the box and the flowers gently placed (face upwards) on the collars. The stems are taped to the cotton wool to reduce any possibility of movement. The blooms can now be transported to the show.

Staging

The ideal way of staging cut blooms is on a staging board or box which allows a 9in square for each bloom. The boards, made from plywood or hardboard, have a front height of 3in and a rear height of 6in. They are made to the following recommended sizes:

1 cut bloom	9in square
3 cut blooms	9in × 27in
6 cut blooms	18in × 27in
12 cut blooms	36in × 27in

The boards should be spray-painted black or covered with material of the same colour. Circular holes cut in the boards accommodate plastic beakers, the rims of which should stand ^{1}2-^{3}4in above the boards. The beakers are filled to within 1in of the top with clean, tepid water. There are those exhibitors who believe that a solution containing 1.8oz (50g) cane sugar, 0.2oz (6g) alum and 1 teaspoon (6ml) sodium hypochlorite (Milton) per gallon of water greatly helps in retaining freshness in the blooms.

When staging, the stem of the bloom should be shortened to about 3in and the cut made at an acute angle so that the cut surface is as large as possible. The bloom is gently placed so that the dorsal petals are resting on the lip of the beaker with the stem in the liquid. A label carrying the name of the cultivar must be placed near to and clearly identifying the bloom.

The Exhibit

Assuming, of course, that the cultivars do conform to the class schedule, there are a number of points to be borne in mind when entering a cut bloom class. It really is essential that there are no obvious faults with the individual blooms, e.g. there are none with multi-centres, deformed petals, colour blotching etc. Every effort should be made to match the sizes of blooms in any one exhibit — most begonia judges place much emphasis on the uniformity of the bloom size. In England the judges are permitted to remove blooms from the containers to examine the back petals — this should always be borne in mind.

Considerable care should be taken in selecting the cultivars to be used in a multi-bloom class. For example, it would be unwise to choose, say, six pale-coloured flowers for a six bloom class. Unless there is a statement in the schedule to the contrary, judges are better disposed towards the exhibitor who has used the maximum choice available, i.e. in the example above, six distinctly different cultivars. In this respect it is unwise to put two blooms of the same cultivar on the same board since this invites the judges to make a comparison between the two. This comparison alone relegates one bloom to be somewhat inferior. In a six cut bloom and a twelve cut bloom class it may help to place the stronger colours towards the rear of the exhibit since this concentrates attention away from the weaker colours at the front. While scarlet-red blooms look most attractive one should be very careful about using deep crimson blooms in a mixed colour class, since they have a pronounced tendency to 'drag' colour out of adjacent blooms thus creating the effect of 'holes' on the board.

A number of three cut bloom classes are colour classes, i.e. three white, three red, three picotee etc. As indicated above, assuming size and quality to be the same, three different cultivars would rate higher than three identical ones.

Whatever the quality of the exhibit, be prepared to experiment with the arrangement of the blooms to obtain what to you is the best balanced, most pleasing arrangement. It is important to remember, however, that when moving blooms around the board great care should be exercised to avoid water dripping on to them.

Pot Plant Classes

Pot plant classes are usually classified as one pot, three pots, six pots and nine or twelve pots and are not 'arranged for effect'. It is therefore, the individual plant quality which is paramount, but one has to be pragmatic and note that while the judges can easily move a single pot and examine it from all angles this is not at all easy with multi-pot classes. Unless, therefore, there are Society rules to the contrary, it is better to grow a single pot as an all round specimen plant and those intended for classes of six pots or more with flowers roughly facing in the same direction. The decision as to which type of plant to grow will be made when the growths from the tuber are some 3-4in high.

As a general guide, a plant intended for entry in the single pot class should have at least three main stems with the leaf tips pointing towards the rim of the pot and at 120° to each other. The final potting should aim to be in a 9-10in pot and the top of the tuber should be placed about $2\frac{1}{2}$in down from the rim of the pot. As with all pot plant classes not more than one tuber is permitted in one pot. Two or three side-shoots should be left on each stem and the objective will be to develop the plant so that the side-shoots are about 12in long some four weeks before the show date. Each plant must be given plenty of bench space so that there is sufficient air circulation to maintain healthy growth. Full ventilation is needed with as much light as possible. Immediately after final potting each main stem must be staked, the positions of the stakes being such as to open up the centre of the plant. Plants intended for the mid-August and early September shows in Britain should be started in March. As soon as the plants have settled into their final pots it is a good idea to give them a spray with a systemic fungicide such as Benomyl. This preventative spray is especially relevant if the grower lives in an area where attacks of powdery mildew are fairly frequent. If the plant does become infected by this fungus then an immediate change to Dinocap is called for.

Plants intended for the multi-pot classes should finish with as many flowers facing forwards as possible. The chosen plants should have at least two main stems, the leaves of which are inclined at 60° to each other. Two or three strong side-shoots will make a potentially ideal plant for these classes. Top dressing the plants should be attended to as roots penetrate the surface of the compost.

Feeding

In principle, feeding pot plants should be no different from that adopted for the cut bloom plants. Maybe for the first few weeks after final potting a balanced 20:20:20 feed could be used to get the plant really growing away, but this should be replaced by a 15:15:30 formulation. Feeding, which should be at one-quarter recommended strength, should be given at three out of every four waterings. The fourth application of clear water helps to remove any deposited salts which might build up in the compost.

Once again it must be emphasised that it is consistent growing during these five or six months of cultivation which will do more than all the 'magic formulae' to achieve a high level of attainment. Perhaps the most important issue is the consistency of watering, of having a compost that is neither too wet nor too dry.

All flower buds which appear should be removed until about

eight weeks before the show date. Four weeks before the show all plants should be checked and any buds which are larger than 2in across should be removed. All growing tips, including side-shoots, should be pinched out. Though the time taken for a bud to reach maximum flower potential varies from one cultivar to another, it will also depend upon the type of weather experienced in the last four weeks. If the weather turns cool and dull it may well be that the 2in buds are fully open on show day, but if it is warm and sunny then the large buds will have gone past their best. This represents the element of luck upon which one always depends when trying to produce quality plants for a fixed show date.

Once again the precautions about watering plants in flower and atmospheric humidity already discussed are equally relevant.

With a number of named cultivars there is a pronounced tendency for the flower buds to be buried within or hidden by the foliage. Some two weeks before the show, efforts should be made to allow the flowers and buds to develop unhindered. A few (three or four) leaves may be removed if it is absolutely necessary, but this should be kept to an absolute minimum. For a multi-pot class the aim is to produce up to twenty-four blooms in a fan-like display and lying within a 160° arc. Any buds which are clearly not going to produce a forward-facing flower can be gently persuaded to do so if the task is begun early enough. Flower supports placed under the neck of the buds can be used successfully in this act of persuasion.

Transportation

There is little doubt that begonia pot plants are a problem when it comes to transportation. The thick stems are easily broken and begonia blooms bruise even when they touch other plant material. Nevertheless, it does seem shortsighted to expend so much effort on growing plants to perfection only to damage them considerably in the space of a few hours. With good planning and careful attention to detail, damage can be reduced to an acceptable minimum. The two major items requiring attention are, first, to wrap every bloom and bud in a thin layer of cotton wool and, second, to ensure the stability of the pot. Several approaches to this second issue have been made — one popular method is to construct wooden boxes of a size at least 4in bigger than the pot size, e.g. an 8in-pot would require a 12in × 23in box. The pot is placed in the box which is then filled with wet sand.

B. 'Yellow Melody' Hiemalis.

B. 'Masquerade' Tuberhybrida,
large flowered double.

B. 'Red Tracery' rhizomatous.

B. 'Merry Christmas' Rex.

B. 'Sweet Dreams' Tuberhybrida, large flowered double.

B. 'Flamingo' Hiemalis.

B. 'Full Moon' Tuberhybrida, large flowered double.

B. 'Scherzo' rhizomatous.

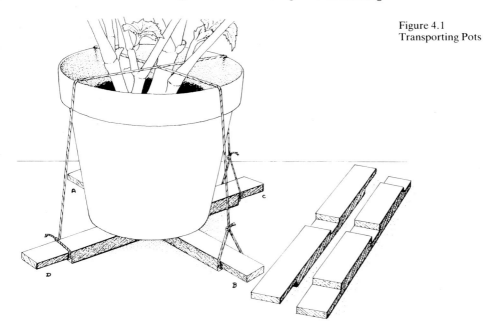

Figure 4.1
Transporting Pots

An alternative, and very successful, method is that devised by Dr David Richardson, a twice awarded British Champion in pot plant classes. A simple wooden support is made from six pieces of $1\frac{3}{8}$in × $\frac{3}{8}$in timber and cut to the following sizes:

    1 × $14\frac{1}{2}$in
    2 × $4\frac{3}{4}$in
    2 × $6\frac{3}{4}$in
    1 × $10\frac{3}{4}$in

Using $\frac{1}{4}$in panel pins two sections are made from the above pieces. The two sections are then slotted together in the form of a cross and the pot is placed symmetrically over the centre. Strong twine is looped over points 'A' and 'D' and the loose ends taken over the rim of the pot and secured at 'B' and 'C' respectively. This procedure firmly attaches the pot to the wooden support which, having dimensions greater than those of the pot thus confers great stability to the pot plant.

Immediately prior to transportation, it is advisable to lower each bloom support slightly to release tension on the flower stems; otherwise the unavoidable movement may well sever the flower heads. Of the two common types of flower support presently available, the model with the soft plastic stirrup and stainless steel leaf spring is by far the best one to use. Both types are available in three sizes, i.e. 10in extending to 15in, 14in extending to 22in and 20in extending to 34in.

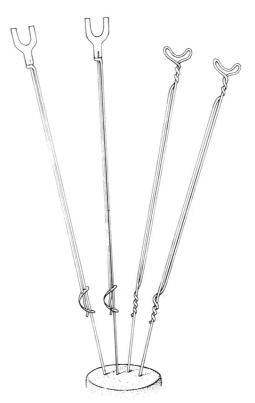

Figure 4.2 Bloom
Supports — Right-
hand Side, Old
Type; Left-hand
Side, New Type with
Stainless Steel
Springs

Staging

Having arrived at the show and unloaded the plants, the first
thing to do is to ascertain exactly where the plant exhibits are to
be staged. A considerable amount of damage to blooms can be
caused if plants have to be manhandled unprotected around the
show.

All the cotton wool can now be removed from the blooms
and, where necessary, the flower supports can be lengthened.

The decision on which plants to enter in a particular class
must be taken with careful reference to the show schedule, but
there are certain guidelines which can be given to those
unfamiliar with begonia competition.

A single pot entry should have an all round bloom effect and,
preferably, the flowers should not all be at the same level.
Blooms at different heights create the effect of depth to the

plant, which also should have an ample supply of clean, healthy foliage. Of course, unhealthy, yellow leaves should be removed, but if their removal gives a bareness to the base of the plant then it is doubtful whether this is a suitable entry in such a class.

Very occasionally the odd leaf obscures a bloom — it is usually possible to persuade such an offender to take up a less prominent position — if not then the leaf may be removed.

By careful observation and even more careful handling, the exhibitor should attempt to space the flowers as uniformly as possible, trying to ensure that no large gaps are left between blooms. Bloom supports should be adjusted so that all blooms 'stare you in the face'. Make certain that all side buds to the male flowers have been removed, as well as all dead and decaying vegetation. This practice of removing all the flanking buds is one which is normal in Britain and the only justification for it is that it does help to increase the male bloom size. One could argue, however, that the full beauty of a plant is only seen when the female flowers are left intact.

Make certain that the pot is clean, a thin layer of fresh compost is spread on the surface and that the correct cultivar name is on the label.

When staging in a pot class it helps not to place a cultivar of a pale shade next to or behind another of a much stronger colour. Of course this is not always possible, but it is better to use plants of a similar strength of colour close to each other.

Where the class schedule calls for multi-pots, the first objective should be to match plants grown in containers of similar size. The plants should display their blooms, or as many as possible, in an arc of 160°, almost fan shaped, again with 'depth'. It is noticeable that, as with the cut blooms, the deep crimson varieties 'drag' colour out of adjacent plants. In this respect the scarlet-reds are to be preferred. It is normal to stage three pots either 'in line' or a 'two and one array'. Six pots are usually placed in two ranks of three, or more occasionally staggered 'three, two and one'. With any of these arrangements it is advantageous to place a very strong colour, e.g. orange or red, at the back of the entry to act as a focal point to the judge. When staging multi-pots it is the practice to raise those at the rear slightly, not for the artistic effect, but simply to enable those plants to be seen.

With all pot plants, the supporting stakes should not protrude above the foliage and every effort should be made to hide their presence, and that of any tying material. In these classes the pots should remain uncovered.

Group Classes

Two types of group class are commonly found in begonia shows. One usually specifies a number of pots, but adds that ferns and foliage plants may be used 'to finish off'. The second type of class is one which does not limit the number of pots and which allows the use of ferns and other foliage plants to be 'used for effect'. The two classes require a somewhat different approach, starting of course with the need to grow slightly different plants.

The first type of group is best served by plants which have been grown in 7in pots on the principle of a main stem with two strong side-shoots. At the peak of perfection this should produce about nine fully open flowers nicely arranged to give the maximum colour effect. The schedule will normally specify the area which may be used to accommodate the plants, e.g. 6ft × 4ft on three-tier staging. The number of pots will usually be twenty. The practice adopted is to place a very strong colour at the centre of the top tier and at such a height that the plants next to it are at a slightly lower level. Taking an imaginary line from this plant down to the mid-point of the bottom tier, the plants are then balanced, in size and in colour tone, on each side of this line. Every effort must be made to avoid obvious gaps or 'dead zones' between the pots, any spaces being filled with foliage, e.g. fern or bracken. Viewed from the front, the whole exhibit should display a slight mound effect, while from the side the flowers should have a sharp wedge shape. All pots should be watered before finishing off the exhibit.

The second type of group is treated differently since the objective here is not simply to have a solid mass of colour as in the previous example, but rather to have larger quantities of foliage material filling in the areas between the colour islands of the begonias. It is customary to assemble together one or two pots of identical cultivars rather than to have a lot of flowers on one plant. Frequently, small plants grown in 5in-pots may be used and these may be assembled at different heights to give depth to the individual cultivar. In principle, the aim is to produce the same wedge-shaped display as before. The two back corners are often occupied by hanging basket begonias.

Rex begonias and semperflorens are, together with coleus, popular plants used to finish off the front of the display.

Judging Tuberous Double Begonias

As with most horticultural subjects, the judging of begonias, whether cut blooms, pot plants or group displays, is one which must involve a great deal of personal preference. It is, therefore, very desirable that the judge(s) should have had a reasonably long acquaintance with and experience of begonias to be able to assess the relative merits of plants and flowers. Nevertheless, the National Begonia Society does have 'Rules for Judging Tuberous Double Begonias' which should also be a most useful guideline for growers and prospective exhibitors.

These rules are subdivided into those which apply to pot plants, to cut blooms and to groups of begonias. They are as follows:

1   Pot Plants
(a)   Ten points for the standard of cultivation. There should be a nice balance between the height and the width of the plant. Blooms need not be spaced all round the plants. Foliage should be healthy and unblemished, loss of leaves will be penalised, but the removal of leaves near to the blooms which are removed to give a better view of the blooms will not be penalised so long as only a minimal number are removed.
(b)   Twenty points for number, quality and size of blooms. Blooms should be fresh with no signs of ageing. Any marks or damage will be penalised. Blooms should be of good size for the variety, if known. The ideal bloom should be circular in outline when viewed from the front and the petals should be symmetrically arranged to give an even-shaped bloom (a rosebud or camellia centre). A divided or uneven centre will be penalised. Ideally each bloom should be of good depth. Blotched blooms of a self coloured variety will be penalised as will any abnormality. Blooms should be held clear of the foliage.
(c)   If more than one pot is called for in the class, five additional points for the staging.
(d)   Each pot to contain only one tuber (this does not apply to hanging baskets).

2   Cut Blooms
(a)   Five points for each bloom for quality and size of bloom. Blooms should be fresh with no signs of ageing. Any marks or damage will be penalised. Blooms should be of good size for the variety if known. The ideal bloom should be circular in outline when viewed from the front and the petals symmetrically arranged to give an even-shaped bloom (rosebud or camellia centred). A divided or uneven centre will be penalised. Ideally each bloom should be of good depth. Blotched blooms of a self coloured variety will be penalised, as will any other abnormality.

(b)   A sixth of the points possible under 2a may be awarded for the staging and variety of colours.

3   Groups of Begonias staged for effect

(a)   Twenty points for general arrangement for effect, harmonious blending of colours etc. Faults: obtrusive pots, stakes etc., overcrowding, uneven staging with plants 'sitting up or down'.

(b)   Ten points for the number, quality and size of blooms.

These rules, while giving some guidance to both exhibitors and judges alike do, nevertheless, leave much to the personal likes and dislikes of those nominated to judge. As prospective exhibitors we must all accept that judges are selected on their fitness to decide on the relative merits of the various entries. It would be sensible to consider the relative importance of a number of faults which are frequently observed with begonias. The comments which follow are personal ones and must not be construed as being universally acceptable.

Bloom Quality

Many of today's cultivars are quite capable of producing individual blooms of 9-10in in diameter and up to 8in in depth. In some instances, however, this size is obtained only at the cost of quality, and it is this resulting 'coarseness' which should be penalised. In many examples this coarseness is easy for all to see and penalties can be fairly applied. Unfortunately there are other aspects of coarse blooms which are less easy to define and about which not all growers would agree. For example, the texture of the petals of most begonias is smooth, almost velvety and the veins complement the colour. Grossly overfed blooms lose their fine texture and frequently the veins become very prominent thus changing the whole character of the flower. This type of coarseness is more difficult to penalise fairly.

A suggestion would be to deduct from the five points awarded to each cut bloom the following penalties.

(i)   Two points for multi or divided centre.
(ii)   One-and-a-half points for blotching in self colours and colour run in picotees.
(iii)   One point for the appearance of adventitious growths or 'warts' between petals.
(iv)   Half a point for ovality in the bloom, roughness in the petals, any minor petal distortion or slight travel damage.

(v)   Half a point for damaged or removed back petals or for aged or flat blooms.

(vi)   If an 8in diameter bloom is taken as about standard add one point for each extra 1in in diameter.

In general, pot plants will produce smaller blooms for the variety but, with that proviso, the above suggestions could still apply. Referring solely to the standard of cultivation of each pot, the maximum of ten points may be penalised as follows:

(i)   Two points for the removal of, say, two lower leaves, with a larger deduction for more leaves.

(ii)   Two points for yellow leaves or for foliage damaged, discoloured or scorched.

(iii)   Five points for plants which are seriously affected by pest or disease.

(iv)   Where the number, size and quality of blooms are concerned, the twenty points might well be allocated to a plant with about 27-30 blooms fully open. Plants with, say, 18-27 blooms might be penalised by three points, with an additional three point penalty for only 12-18 blooms.

Multi centres are not usually a problem with pot plants, but bloom size frequently is. Taking 6in as standard bloom size and adding one point for each extra 1in diameter might be reasonable.

It must be stressed that the above are only suggestions intended to help the exhibitor make relative decisions about his/her own plants. In no way do they reflect any official view of which the author is aware. Most judges eliminate exhibits initially on an 'appreciation' basis and then apply a more rigorous pointing approach to the final decision on placings.

While the preceding remarks might sound a little formidable to the novice begonia grower, they should not inhibit or discourage anyone from competition. There is nothing which will do more for the raising of growing standards than healthy competitive showing. The following cultivars are suggested as suitable subjects for exhibiting.

For Pot Plants:

White or Cream	'Diana Wynyard'
	'Avalanche'
	'Buttermilk'
	'Full Moon'
Yellow	'Majesty'

	'Midas'
	'Festiva'
Red	'Scarlet O'Hara'
	'Sceptre'
	'Crown Prince'
	'Bonfire'
	'Alan Langdon'
Pink	'Rosalind'
	'Carmen'
	'Falstaff'
	'Roy Hartley'
	'Sugar Candy'
	'Sweet Dreams'
	'Judy Langdon'
Picotee	'Wedding Day'
	'Fred Martin'
	'Fairylight'
	'Masquerade'
	'Coronet'
Orange	'Zoe Colledge'
	'City of Ballarat'
	'Tahiti'

For Cut Blooms

White or Cream	'Full Moon'
	'Snowbird'
	'Avalanche'
	'Bernat Klein'
Yellow	'Midas'
	'Primrose'
Orange	'City of Ballarat'
	'Tahiti'
	'Zoe Colledge'
	'Hawaii'
Red	'Red Admiral'
	'Scarlet O'Hara'
	'Allan Langdon
Picotee or Bicolour	'Peach Melba'
	'Bali Hi'
	'Wedding Day'
	'Can Can'
	'Masquerade'
	'Fred Martin'
	'Fairylight'

CHAPTER 5

Propagation

Two methods of increasing stock are available to the begonia grower: seed production or vegetative propagation. These two methods assume very different degrees of importance depending upon whether the grower is primarily interested in species or in cultivars. For example, all the large-flowered tuberous double begonias grown today are cultivars with many years of hybridisation behind them. With these and all other cultivars, vegetative propagation is the only way to increase the stock of identical plants. On the other hand, self-pollinated species produce seed from which plants identical to the parents can be raised. For convenience, this chapter will deal first with the propagation methods applied to the tuberous begonias and then those which are relevant to the non-tuberous types.

There have been occasional reports from growers who claim to have propagated tuberous begonias successfully using cut leaves as vegetative material. While it is difficult to state categorically that no such propagation can occur (or at least to provide a viable plant for the following year), it does seem strange that the method has never enjoyed universal success. The most common method of propagation is by cuttings, but there are a number of variations even on this theme which will be discussed below. It must be said that in almost all known examples of this type of propagation the new plant is an exact replica of the parent — there are, however, one or two isolated cases of mutations occurring.

Tuberous Begonias

Cuttings may be of two types, basal and stem. The basal type is available in the early and late season, and they usually root very easily, whereas stem cuttings are normally available mid-season. The ease of rooting stem cuttings is related to the softness of growth, since there is a pronounced tendency for rotting to occur with plants which have been grown too soft.

Basal Cuttings

Begonia tubers which are three or four years old often produce
four or five growth shoots when started in the spring. Shoots in
excess of two or three may be removed and used as cuttings. In
a similar way basal shoots are often produced late in the season
after the plants have been stopped. It is better to wait until the
shoot is 2-3in high before removing it. Careful examination of
the base of the shoot will reveal an embryonic bud or 'eye' —
not infrequently more than one eye will be found at the base.
When removing the shoot it is essential that this bud is attached
and undamaged. A very sharp bladed knife or scalpel is the best
tool for excising the cutting. The cutting tool should be
sterilised by dipping it into methylated or surgical spirit, thus
lessening the chance of spreading any disease from plant to
plant. Having located an 'eye', the growth is severed by a clean
cut below this point. One frequently hears the suggestion that if
a small section of the tuber is removed, together with the
cutting, then rooting will be that much easier. This is quite

Figure 5.1
Equipment for
Taking Cuttings

erroneous and the practice should be discouraged. As we have noted, there are a number of eyes around the basal cutting and as many of these as possible should be kept intact on the tuber. Next year's growths often start around the base of the present year's growth so as much of the tuber around this area should remain undamaged.

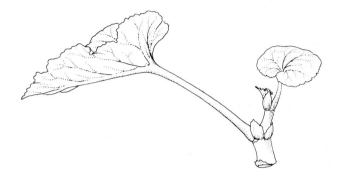

Figure 5.2 Stem Cuttings with 'Eye'

The presence of the embryonic shoot bud ensures plant growth for the following season. The small tuber which will come from this cutting retains the 'eye' within it and from it will come next year's growth. A damaged 'eye' will not prevent the formation of a tuber, but this is unlikely to start up next year. Occasionally a cutting does not form a tuber by the end of the growing season, but this does not necessarily mean that the cutting has been wasted. In many instances, when the stem falls

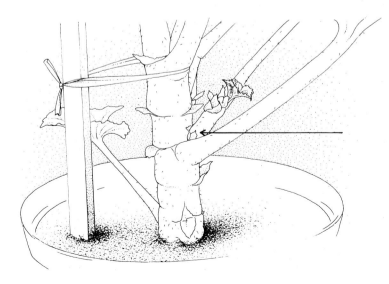

Figure 5.3 Stem Cutting Ready for Removal — Note Bract which Protects the 'Eye'

away, a small section (up to the first node) remains attached to the root system. It is at this node that a leaf stem has been attached when the cutting was in growth. In the leaf axil there was almost certainly an undeveloped growth bud which would remain there when the stem had fallen away. This small stem section will start up in the spring and produce a good plant. Tuberless cuttings such as described are often produced from the late basal shoots. These cuttings have to be grown on through the winter in heat and never subjected to the lower temperatures necessary for the production of tubers.

Stem Cuttings

The other type of cutting is that taken as a side-shoot from the main stem of the plant. Unless the plant is being cultivated to produce cut blooms it is usual to retain the lower one or two side-shoots for flowering. Above these, side-shoots appear at each leaf axil and may be used as cuttings. The problem for every grower is, of course, to balance the need to propagate the plants (and hence cover any losses in overwintering) against the requirement to produce a well proportioned flowering plant. Removal of these cuttings is not always easy due to the restriction of space with certain varieties. Taking the sterilised knife or scalpel, two cuts are made, one vertical and parallel to the main stem, and the other below the cutting and at right angles to the main stem. This will result in a wedge-shaped base to the cutting which can now be gently removed. Once again, great care should be exercised to ensure that the 'eye' at the base of the cutting remains intact and undamaged — an adventitious slip with the scalpel can almost decapitate the plant. An alternative, and safer, method is to allow the side-shoot to develop further before taking the cutting. If one examines the junction of the first leaf on the side-shoot an 'eye' will often be found here. The cut can then be made just below this leaf joint and, after removing the cutting, the leaf stem is carefully trimmed away. After removing cuttings of any type it is sensible to dust the wound with green sulphur.

Rooting
Cuttings

A number of well tried methods are available for the rooting of cuttings and unless the begonia grower masters at least one of them his or her hobby is going to prove a most expensive one.

The cuttings may be rooted in a loam-based compost of John Innes No. 1 formulation, in sharp silver sand, in a mixture of equal parts peat and silver sand or in plain water. In Chapter 3 we noted that begonias prefer a compost of pH 6.5-6.8, and it would, therefore, be reasonable to add a small amount of ground chalk to the sand/peat mixture to correct its high acidity.

A 2in plastic pot is loosely filled with the chosen rooting medium which is slightly moist. The cutting is dipped into a rooting hormone powder (preferably one which contains a fungicide), and then inserted to a depth of 1in into the medium close to the side of the pot. If the cutting is simply pushed into the compost there is a chance that the 'eye' will be damaged so it is wise to make a small hole. The compost is gently firmed around the cutting and the pot placed in a propagator at 65-70°F (18-21°C). Under ideal conditions rooting should take some three weeks. It is these 'ideal conditions' which cause so many difficulties and there are a number of approaches which can be tried.

Mist Propagation

If mist is available then the propagator will be open at all times. The leaves of the cuttings remain wet at all times and no flagging takes place. The base temperature should never fall below 70°F (21°C), otherwise there is a distinct chance that rotting will take place rather than rooting. The propagator should be placed where plenty of light, but not direct sunlight, can reach the plants. During misting, a loss of chlorophyll is often noticed, though this is quickly replaced during the subsequent growth. Personal experience with tuberous begonias has never indicated the need to 'wean' the rooted cuttings. Success with the late-rooted basal cuttings is more likely if mist is available.

No Mist

One of the major causes for the loss of cuttings is the onset of rot, and frequently the fault lies in using a supply of unclean water. In the absence of mist, a closed propagator should be used. If the greenhouse is a glass to ground model then under the bench is a convenient place to site the propagator. The pots are placed on a sand bed maintained at 65-70°F (18-21°C) and the top almost closed during sunny periods, but open when dull or during the night. This procedure is followed in an attempt to maintain atmospheric humidity around the cuttings. If the humidity falls, the leaves transpire moisture into the air, thus causing the cuttings to flag. The sand bed is kept wet at all times, and a periodic light spray of clean water over the leaves is beneficial. If the propagator is kept permanently closed then there is a high probability that the cuttings will rot.

Plastic Bags

If no propagator is available then it is sometimes possible to root the cuttings by placing the pot and cutting into a plastic bag, which is then securely closed. The bag and contents are then hung in the apex of the greenhouse, but out of the direct rays of the sun. The extra warmth in the upper part of the greenhouse assists the rooting process. Personal experience with this method has not been too successful since, with the falling night temperature, condensation occurs in the bag and the leaves adhere to the walls; rotting of the leaves seems to follow rapidly. Other growers, however, claim this to be a most successful method.

Rooting in Water

In recent years there has been an increase in the rooting of cuttings by simply placing the lower 1in of stem in clean water. The small, narrow-necked, clear glass tablet bottles of some $\frac{1}{2}$oz (10ml) capacity are ideal for this purpose. Some people like to add a little feed to the water, but this is quite

Figure 5.4 Cuttings in Plastic Bags

unnecessary. The bottle and cutting are placed in a well lit place at about 65°F (18°C). Small roots will ultimately appear at the base of the cutting. When these are about ¼in long, the cutting should be potted up in a peat-based compost and grown on in the usual way. If the roots are allowed to get too long, then considerable losses are experienced when the transfer to the compost is carried out.

Cuttings may be taken and rooted at any time during the growing season. Basal cuttings taken at the beginning of the year root very quickly and may produce exhibition quality blooms from 5in-pots late in the year. Cuttings taken in mid to late season (June/October in Britain) should be grown on as long as possible into the following year (February/March in Britain) and for this they will require warmth. They will probably need to be repotted into 4in pots and will benefit from an occasional feed with a 20:20:20 fertiliser. When they are growing away well, the growth tip should be pinched out — this has the effect of producing a tuber which is, in effect, a two-year-old one. Cuttings taken from high up on the stem often do not root quite so readily as those from lower down, and there is always the possibility, though remote, that mutants are produced.

Tuber Division

This propagation method is not highly recommended, but it may be used when circumstances demand. This could be the scarcity value of the tuber or it could be that the tuber has become very big and is not readily accommodated in a 8-9in pot. As we have already seen, such tubers often produce a number of growths. These should be allowed to develop until they are about 1in high. The tuber may now be cut up into sections each carrying one shoot, though what is much more important is that each section must have a root system. The cut surface should be dusted with a mixture of orthocide and green sulphur, or with charcoal. When potting the cut sections, the compost should be kept away from the cut surface for two weeks or so to allow complete drying to take place. It must be remembered that this technique should not be repeated the following year since roots will never be produced from the cut surface.

Tissue Culture

The propagation of begonias by cuttings, though producing additional plants identical to the parent, is a slow process. For

101

the amateur grower who might need only five or six plants of any one cultivar, this meets his or her needs adequately. For the commercial grower, however, there are obviously disadvantages in that the period between selecting a particular cross and building up the necessary stocks for release, could be as long as nine years. It also means that a new cross which has certain special features, e.g. a new colour break, but which does not produce many side-shoots, may never reach the stage of exploitation.

It is also the case that, as the years go by, most begonia tubers become more infected by bacteria. In these circumstances it must be questionable whether any new begonia release which has come via the cutting propagation method, ever fully realises its true potential. Primarily because of the time delay in producing adequate stocks, exacerbated by the high cost of labour, alternative and more economical propagation methods have been sought. For many years now, following the pioneering work of Professor Morel and others, an increasing number of horticultural subjects, e.g. potatoes, rhubarb, soft fruits, bulbs, orchids etc., have been successfully propagated by the laboratory culture of minute plant sections on sterile media. In many instances the objective of such work has been to eradicate virus from the plant material, thus enhancing the yield and quality of the product. The eradication of virus has required the excision of a minute portion of the growing tip, known as a meristem. In the case of tuberous double begonias, which are not known to be virused, it is unnecessary to excise such a small amount of tissue. The usual practice is to remove the top $\frac{1}{8}$in portion of an embryonic growth bud which is low down on the plant. The 'explant' is sterilised, washed and placed on the surface of a nutrient gel. The composition of the nutrient is such that the explant is encouraged to multiply, a process which takes place under the right conditions of light and temperature. Rates of multiplication vary from plant to plant, but if it were only five per month then it can be readily shown that, after the first division, such a rate could lead to 15,000 offspring in five months.

Transfer of these plantlets to a different medium could then encourage root formation. The 'tissue culture' method has now been developed commercially for tuberous begonias, though it is too early to say whether it is entirely reliable. Certain cultivars do not respond at all well, others are unreliable, behaving well on one occasion but badly on another. All too often, whole batches of plantlets will collapse for no known

B. 'Lucerna' cane-stemmed.

B. 'Venus' Tuberhybrida, large flowered double.

B. 'City of Ballaarat' Tuberhybrida, large flowered double.

B. 'Snowbird' Tuberhybrida, large flowered double.

B. 'Red Admiral' Tuberhybrida, large flowered double.

B. 'Can-Can' Tuberhybrida, large flowered picotee.

B. 'Aphrodite Pink' Hiemalis.

B. 'Baluga' Hiemalis.

reason. Much more work needs to be done in this field and particularly on discovering which is the most reliable tissue to take, but it is undoubtedly the propagation method of the future. One of the clear advantages of the tissue method is that it supplies new cultivars to the amateur before the parent plant has become too infected with bacteria. It could be that one of the future developments will be to supply customers with new stock of the same variety every year and at a low price.

Whether this method can be adapted for use by the amateur remains to be seen, but the equivalent situation in the orchid world is that many semi-professionals now successfully operate meristem propagation methods.

Seed Propagation

The propagation of begonias from seed is not very common, and the method is reserved for reproduction of begonia species by self pollination and for the mass production of unnamed tuberous begonias for bedding purposes. The mass displays of semperflorens begonias in our gardens and public parks use plants raised from F1 hybrid seed. The growing of begonias from seed has been adequately dealt with in Chapter 3. The crossing of hybrids and cultivars produces plants which may be similar, but not identical, to the parents. The production of seed is, of course, an essential part of the search for new cultivars, but that will be dealt with in Chapter 6.

Non-Tuberous Begonias

The majority of the non-tuberous begonias are propagated by either stem or leaf cuttings. The former are used almost exclusively for the cane-stemmed, shrub-like and rhizomatous types. Leaf cuttings are used for Rex begonias as well as the rhizomatous types. This division must not be taken too rigorously, but it is a convenient classification for our use. As with the tuberous double begonias most growers appear to have their favourite rooting medium, but a suitable mix to start with, and which is generally acceptable to both types is:

1 part by volume sphagnum peat
1 part by volume Perlite (seedling grade)

This is a sterile medium which has the important feature of being an open compost giving good drainage — essential for good rooting.

Stem Cuttings

The cane-stemmed and shrub-like begonias are best propagated by this method. The tip stem cuttings are taken preferably from young growths rather than the old, hard stems. At each leaf joint there is a node, and where possible the cutting should be taken at a point just below it. The tip cutting should be 2-3in long, though with some of the larger leaved varieties it is difficult to avoid taking 4-5in tips. The cut should be made at an angle to the stem to increase the area of the rooting surface. The tip cutting is then inserted into the rooting medium to a depth at which it will remain upright against the rim of the pot. With some of the more substantial cane-stemmed begonias it may be necessary to remove the lower leaves to obtain the required depth of insertion. The use of hormone rooting powders is one about which there are differences of opinion. They do not act as 'magic potions', but when rooting is going to take place, a hormone powder will speed the process.

Occasionally, and especially with certain varieties, there may be surplus basal shoots which can also be rooted successfully as above. B. Semperflorens, the Hiemalis and Rieger begonias may also be propagated by removing a stem tip carrying three nodes. It is helpful, but by no means essential, to provide bottom heat to speed the rooting process, 60°F (15.6°C) being adequate. A few of the more delicate species might need a closed environment for successful propagation — this can easily be accommodated by placing the container in a closed plastic bag.

Most of the cane-stemmed and shrub-like stem cuttings will root readily within three weeks by simply placing them in clean water. As with the tuberous begonias, the root system so developed does not always transplant easily into a compost — they should be potted up as soon as the tiny roots are seen. When properly rooted, the cuttings should be potted on into 3-4in pots and in a compost consisting of:

3 parts by volume sphagnum peat
1 part by volume Perlite
1 part by volume sharp grit

To this mixture should be added a small amount of base fertiliser. After potting, the cutting should be placed in a position out of direct sunlight until it is firmly established and growing away.

Rhizome Cuttings

The majority of the non-tuberous begonias popular in Britain
are of the Rex and rhizomatous types. Propagation is very

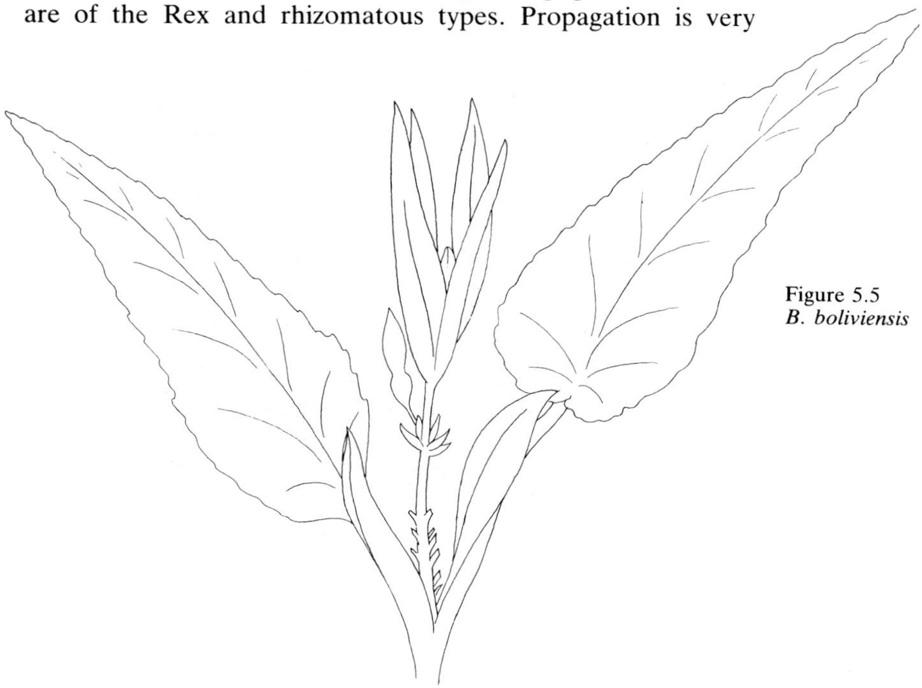

Figure 5.5
B. boliviensis

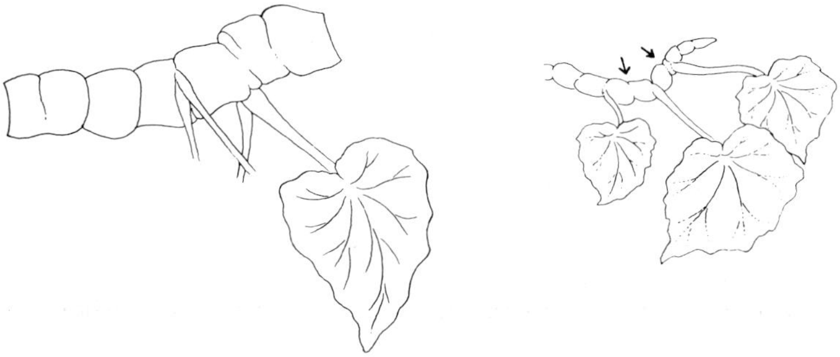

Figure 5.6
Rhizome Cuttings

easily achieved by using rhizome cuttings. Since a rhizome is only a thickened or enlarged stem, the method may be considered as a special example of a stem cutting. Depending upon the state of the plant, two types of rhizome cutting can be taken. If there is a considerable degree of branching with the rhizome, then one or more of these stem tips can be spared for propagation. The rhizome tip bearing two nodes is removed with a sharp scalpel; the cutting is then dipped into rooting hormone and inserted into the compost to a depth of $\frac{1}{2}$-1in.

Figure 5.7 Leaf
Cuttings

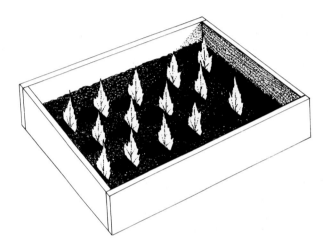

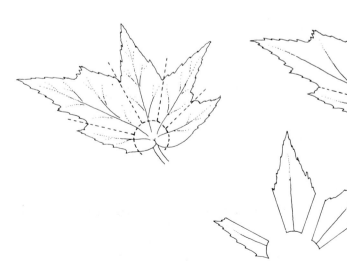

If a larger specimen can be spared then a piece some 2in long, but carrying leaves, is removed and cut up into sections, each section carrying a leaf. The sections are placed on the surface of the compost and lightly covered, the leaves standing clear. The cuttings of both types are placed in the propagator and the compost kept moist; rooting should be in 3-4 weeks.

Leaf Cuttings

Though propagation by rhizome cuttings works very well, many growers seem to be unwilling to sacrifice any of the active stems. A much more common method of propagation of these types is by leaf cuttings. From one rather small leaf it is possible to produce a number of plants identical to the parent. Three slightly different methods are used, all using the same open, free-draining compost.

Whole Leaves

For the very small-leaved begonias, e.g. 'Mac's Gold', a leaf is removed, complete with as much leaf stalk as possible. Cut a clean end to the stalk and insert this into the compost as far as possible with the leaf standing clear of the surface.

Severing Main Veins

For the slightly larger-leaved begonias (up to 2in diameter or width) use the petiole to anchor the leaf on the surface of the compost. The main veins are severed using a sharp knife or scalpel and the leaf pegged flat on to the surface of the medium with small pieces of wire. At the height of the growing season rooting takes place quickly at the severed veins, allowing a number of plantlets to be obtained from a single leaf.

Wedge Cuttings

For the very large-leaved begonias (especially the Rex types) both of the above methods are inconvenient and wedge cuttings are preferable. A section of leaf is removed around the spot where the petiole joins the leaf. The leaf is then cut into wedge-shaped sections, starting the cut at the leaf edge and working back towards the first cut. Each wedge should contain a main vein. The wedges are inserted into the rooting medium to a depth of about one quarter to one half their length. As with all leaf cuttings, the rooting medium must be kept uniformly moist, but not over-wet. Water should only be given by immersing the container, and not by overhead spray.

When rooting has taken place, the small plantlets should be moved on into individual 2in-pots using a mixture of soilless compost and Perlite or grit in the volume proportions of 3:1. Within four weeks a second move into 3in pots will be needed, when the plants can now be treated as mature subjects.

CHAPTER 6

Hybridising

The creation of a new cultivar is the unspoken ambition of many amateur horticulturists, and in this respect, the grower of begonias is not unique.

For the large-flowered tuberous double enthusiast the aim of hybridising is probably to obtain an unusual colour break or extra large flowers or perhaps the perfect rose-shaped bloom. The chances for the amateur to produce something unique is extremely remote. The commercial nurseries raise and flower upwards of 100,000 seedlings each year, the vast majority of which are not considered to be worthwhile for further development. Frequently unnamed stock plants are used in this activity, plants which may be relied upon to confer a special attribute to their progeny. Nevertheless, as with the football pools or a State Lottery, there is always the remote possibility of success, and in any case, the journey is often more exciting than the destination.

Similar remarks can be made concerning the winter flowering begonias of the Hiemalis and Cheimantha groups — they have been extensively exploited by the commercial nurseries.

With the other types of begonia the situation is somewhat different since perhaps the aims are less well defined than with those mentioned above. The possibilities of hybridising are enormous since many types of begonia species, varieties and cultivars are capable of crossing successfully with each other. While it may be of some general interest to cross plants haphazardly, it is much more constructive to work methodically with a fairly specific goal in mind. Perhaps one is attempting to produce an angel-wing begonia which is compact and capable of flowering the year round with panicles of golden yellow flowers. Perhaps it is a Rex begonia with significant flowers or a hardy rhizomatous type. It is well to remember, however, that while the tuberous double hybrids and the semperflorens begonias can be raised, flowered and selected out of doors, many of the other hybrids need to be grown entirely under glass, and that means a lot of greenhouse space. This is particularly the case when the larger cane-stemmed begonias are crossed.

Pollination

With the possible exception of the tuberhybrida group, pollen is fairly readily available, and the male and female flowers easily distinguished. The female flower carries a winged seed pod or ovary just below the petals. The male flower (which frequently falls off before the female opens) is the more spectacular bloom, and with a number of begonias there is a pronounced tendency for the petals to reflex backwards, thus exposing the ripe pollen. The pollen is seen to be ripe when it adheres readily to a camel-hair brush drawn very lightly across the stamens. The pollen is transferred by first removing the male flower and gently removing the petals. Holding the stripped flower by the stem it is then gently brushed over the pistils of the female flower. A soft brush can be used for this purpose, but if more than one cross is being made then the brush should be dipped into methylated spirit and dried after each pollen transfer. If the pollen is ripe and the pistils receptive then seed will set — the female flower petals will fade, close and fall, and the ovary will swell. Within a few weeks the flower stem will shrivel and dry and the seed pod may be removed. It should be kept in a fairly dry place until it is clearly dry or it splits.

It frequently happens that the availability of pollen does not coincide with the most receptive time for the female flower. This may be due to the slightly different flowering periods of the two plants or simply because the male flower of a single plant has opened and fallen off well in advance of the female bloom. If this is a problem then the pollen can be stored in a refrigerator in a closed glass jar until required. The ripe pollen can be easily shaken from the male flower on to waxed paper.

Obtaining seed from cultivars of the modern tuberous double begonias is a much more difficult task, mainly due to the difficulty in obtaining pollen. Such has been the intensive hybridisation with this group, coupled with the search for very large and very double male flowers, that the pollen-bearing stamens have virtually disappeared in modern cultivars. Indeed, any residual stamens present would indicate a flower in which doubling is less than perfect, and with this group this is undesirable. In this never ending quest for fully double flowers, the hybridist is cutting off further development simply by denying himself the means of flower reproduction.

Fortunately, however, small cutting tubers of many cultivars, taken in mid-season and grown on in 3in-pots, will frequently produce single or semi-double male flowers in mid-late autumn. Transfer of pollen is carried out with a sable-hair brush rather than removing the large male bloom. Even under the most favourable conditions far from all modern tuberous double begonias are able to produce pollen and not all female flowers have receptive stigma. For example, there are a number of yellow ground picotees available — 'Coronet', 'Corona', 'Jean Blair', 'Can Can', 'Gillian Davies', 'Seville', 'Jamboree' etc. — but of these, 'Jean Blair' is the only one which will produce pollen at all freely.

During the period of seed setting and the development of the seed pods it is advisable to reduce the greenhouse humidity to about 50 per cent RH with a minimum night temperature of 60°F (15.7°C).

Separating the Seed

As soon as the seed pod has dried or has just begun to split, it is removed and carefully placed on a sheet of white paper in a safe, dry position out of direct sunlight. During the next few days the pod will wither and split open, thus permitting the seed to be shaken out. The contents of the pod will include fertile and infertile seed as well as chaff. The lighter (in weight) infertile seed and chaff can be partly removed by *gently* blowing on the seed. Further cleaning can sometimes be done by gently inclining the paper. Fertile seed should roll down the paper very readily leaving the chaff behind. This process can be helped by tapping the paper. Using a hand magnifying glass it is possible to distinguish viable seed from dust and chaff; one should avoid sowing chaff since it has a pronounced tendency to encourage moulds in the seed pan. The viable seed can be stored, folded in small pieces of tissue, sealed in waxed paper envelopes and stored in the refrigerator (not in the freezing compartment).

Sowing the Seed

The production of plants from seed has already been covered in Chapter 3 and need not be repeated. It is important to note, however, that the viability of begonia seed is reduced the longer it is kept. It is not possible to be definitive about how long any one cross will remain reasonably viable — seed from tuberous double begonias has reduced with acceptable viability certainly two years after hybridisation. Seed from a *B. angularis* self

Figure 6.1 Seedlings
at Various Stages of
Growth (All Seeds
Were Sown at the
Same Time)

crossing had a low (less than 5 per cent) viability after six years, though one or two healthy seedlings were obtained. Good viability with *B. cinnabarina* after four years has been found, but there are reports that with certain species crosses, poor viability was found after only three months.

CHAPTER 7

Pests, Diseases and Cultural Problems

The majority of begonias discussed here are cultivated in an enclosed environment, be it greenhouse, conservatory or the home. There is little doubt that, under these circumstances, proper ventilation, air circulation, atmospheric humidity and plant hygiene will assist considerably in reducing the probability of an attack by pest or disease. Where it is feasible, proper arrangements should be made for an annual disinfection of the growing area by thorough washing down with Jeyes' Fluid, the odourless Consan or a solution of formaldehyde (Steriform). With each of these chemicals it is essential that the plants should be removed and the manufacturer's instructions strictly adhered to.

Begonias, especially the tuberous double types, are very soft and fleshy so that dead leaves or flowers, if left on the benches or pots, can rapidly cause rots and disease to infect otherwise healthy plants. Plant cleanliness is, therefore, of the greatest importance, especially at the end of the growing season. Even when greenhouse and plant cleanliness have been attended to, begonias, though not as susceptible as many other plants, do occasionally suffer from the attentions of pests and disease.

Poor growth techniques may also cause problems, though these are not always easy to diagnose accurately.

The difficulties most frequently encountered may be conveniently treated as those resulting from pests, diseases and cultural disorders.

It cannot be stressed too much that the use of chemicals in the greenhouse, whether they are insecticides, fungicides etc, constitutes a potential danger to humans and animals alike. All these materials should be kept well out of the reach of children and should be properly labelled. The manufacturer's instructions should be carefully read and rigorously adhered to. At any one time sufficient solution for a single application should be prepared and all equipment should be washed immediately after use. Contact with the body, especially the

113

hands and mouth should be avoided but if this does occur then washing with copious amounts of water should be carried out.

Pests

Aphids

It is somewhat surprising that, no matter how severe an aphid attack is during the growing season, one finds generally that it is the begonias which are among the last to be affected. Indeed, many growers of tuberous double begonias have never seen a greenfly on any of their plants. Nevertheless, rare though an attack might be, once it has occurred, the effects can be disastrous. Greenfly are soft-bodied insects which survive by sucking sap from the softer parts of the plant, especially the underside of the leaves and the succulent growing tips. Left untreated, even a mild attack will retard, if not totally stop, the plant development and also cause severe curling of the leaves. In the rather warm, humid atmosphere of the growing environment black sooty moulds can also infect the damaged plant tissue. Since the aphids are immobile, treatment is relatively simple, requiring only a spray with an insecticide based upon HCH (formerly gamma BHC), malathion or pyrethrum. These sprays will not destroy the eggs of the aphids, so that spraying should be continued over a three week period to account for one or two generations. The use of systemic insecticides should be approached with some caution, since a number of formulations on the market are suspected of inhibiting the proper development of young growths. Even HCH should not be used on tubers in the very early stages of growth.

Whitefly

In recent years, this pest, another sap-sucking insect, has become more of a problem to growers of begonias. The incidence of an attack is far greater if the begonias are close to other subjects thought to be almost host plants, e.g. tomatoes, chrysanthemums, berberis etc. The weaker-growing begonias seem to be especially prone to the attentions of whitefly. In the early stages of an infestation one might be forgiven for not noticing the occasional specks of white ash on the leaves or growing tips. When disturbed, the whitefly rise in a small cloud above the plant, rapidly settling back on the leaves.

Whitefly are not easy to eradicate. In the case of a mild attack washing the infected plant with a very dilute detergent solution will be most effective — the pest sticks to the slightly sticky liquid. This treatment will also remove the 'honeydew' which often accompanies an attack and which also encourages the growth of sooty moulds. More severe infestations must be treated with successive applications of a spray containing resmethrin.

Earwigs

Not a common pest, but one, which if allowed to go unchecked will seriously disfigure a plant and render it useless for show purposes. Early evidence of its presence are the circular holes chewed in the leaves; later, when the blooms are opening, this pest has a nasty habit of severing whole petals at their base. With the large-flowered tuberous double begonias, earwigs frequently penetrate deep into the flower when disturbed. One simple method of persuading them to exit peacefully is to blow gently into the flower. The treatment for earwigs is to sprinkle the insecticide Carbaryl (Sevin dust) on the surface of the compost around the main stems.

Mites

These creatures are so small that one usually needs a magnifying lens to see them. Invariably their presence is revealed only when the damage has been done. Included in this group are Begonia mites, red spider mites and thrips (strictly insects).

Begonia mites (Tarsonemus sps.) cause galls and scarring on leaf veins and are probably the major factor in producing 'blindness' in plants. Blindness is the condition where the growing point of the stem ceases to develop.

Red spider mites cause yellowing and browning of the underside of the leaves, especially at the junction of the veins. Frequently the damaged area is covered with tiny spider webs.

Thrips are pale straw-coloured insects (about $\frac{1}{4}$-$\frac{1}{2}$mm in length) which suck the sap from the undersides of the leaves, leaving brown or silvery blotches along the leaf veins. If left unchecked, thrips will ultimately cause severe damage to flower buds and flowers. Frequently the buds are reluctant to open, and when they do the petals are seen to be deformed or streaked with brown.

All of these pests thrive under the dry, arid conditions which can occur in small greenhouses during the hot summer months. Every effort should be made to maintain a high humidity (about 70 per cent) without producing a stagnant atmosphere. Systemic organophosphorous acaricides, e.g. dimethoate (Rogor E), can be very effective, though there is some evidence that these products can themselves result in chemical damage to begonias, espcially to the tuberous types. There is little doubt that in this instance, prevention is better than cure.

An alternative treatment is a spray containing dicofol (Kelthane); Murphy's Combined Pest and Disease Spray contains this active ingredient.

Mealybug

These pests are not common predators on begonias, though attacks can occur especially if other plants in the greenhouse, e.g. lilies, are infected. The mealybug feeds by sucking sap, usually on the main stem or the underside of the leaves, and lays its eggs in fluffy white sacs. It must be remembered that the mealybug may lay its eggs not on the plant but on some nearby object or even on the underside of the greenhouse bench. If detected, the mealybug can cause severe debilitation of the plant, but it also secretes a sticky honeydew which will soon be the site for a black sooty mould. A small attack of mealybug can be dealt with by swabbing the fluffy white sacs with cotton wool saturated with methylated spirit. Heavier infestations will require a forceful spray with malathion or diazinon insecticide (Fison's Combat Insecticide or Gesal Plant Spray).

Fungus Flies

These are also variously known as Moss Flies and Mushroom Flies, but are correctly termed Sciarid Flies. They are very small dark-coloured 'midges' which hover above the surface of the compost. As their name suggests, they are very common where soilless composts are used, but they also congregate around decaying vegetable matter or where high organic nitrogen containing fertilizers, e.g. dried blood, are used. The flies themselves are harmless enough though they hardly enhance the beauty of the plants. Far more serious, however, is the fact that the flies lay their eggs in the root system and the tiny larvae which emerge feed on the plant roots, eventually causing rots to occur. With a severe attack the whole plant might collapse.

One effective control is simply to keep the fly population down to low levels. This is most readily accomplished by hanging solid insecticide strips containing dichlorvos at 8ft intervals in the greenhouse and at bench level (Vapona Fly Killer Strips).

Vine Weevil

For the grower of tuberous begonias, this pest has in the past few years become a major problem and the person who has not experienced at least one infestation is fortunate.

The weevil is a small ($\frac{1}{4}$-$\frac{1}{2}$in long) white grub with a brown head which burrows into the tuber. The parent is a dark grey-brown beetle about $\frac{1}{2}$in long which may lay up to 1,000 eggs on the surface of the tuber in spring and summer. The grubs have insatiable appetites and, within a period of some three months, a complete tuber can be destroyed by their attack. Tunnels bored into the tuber are a sure sign of the attentions of the vine weevil. If the grub is still there then it must be dug out and destroyed. Control or eradication is difficult since the one sure way of killing the grubs is to incorporate a small quantity of Aldrin, a persistent organochlorine insecticide into the compost. This insecticide, though banned from use on edible crops, may still be available for use on ornamental plants.

Figure 7.1 Vine Weevil Beetle, 'Click Beetle'

Alternative treatments which can be tried are to water the compost in the late summer with HCH or to incorporate Bromophos into the compost.

There is no doubt that vine weevil is a most destructive pest, and a careful watch should be kept for any sign of the parent beetle. Cyclamen is a known host plant for the weevil.

Eelworm
The tuberous double and the cane-stemmed begonias are, among all the other groups, the most likely to be the ones which suffer an attack of eelworm. Two forms of this pest have been recognised, tuber eelworm (Meloidogne sps.) and leaf eelworm. The former attacks the tubers, producing groups of small swellings on the surface of the tuber. There is no known treatment for this nematode and the tuber must be destroyed,

together with any cuttings from it and the compost in which it was growing.

Leaf eelworm, like many other nematodes, is a thin worm-like creature too small to be seen with the naked eye. As its name suggests, it is to be found in the leaf tissue of affected plants. Symptoms of an attack can be easily seen by holding a leaf up to the light — the tissue between the main veins is deeper in colour; later it will become brown and, later still, it will turn black and brittle. The infection appears to spread towards the leaf edges. If left untreated the whole plant becomes infected and all the leaves wither and die. The whole plant will collapse eventually.

Leaf eelworm is transmitted readily from one plant to another via the film of moisture which is present where the leaves of adjacent plants touch. There is, therefore, consider-able danger in a whole collection becoming infected. It is possible to eradicate leaf eelworm either by hot water treatment (this may take two or three years to be fully successful) or by chemical treatment (which is very hazardous).

(a) Hot water treatment: When in their dormant stage, the begonias are immersed in water previously heated to *and kept at* 46°F (115°C) for 15 minutes. After treatment, the tubers are placed in cold water for a further 15 minutes. It is often the practice to add a small amount of orthocide to the cold water to help in killing off any moulds which might be on the tuber surface.

(b) Chemical treatment: Aldicarb (Temik) is a most effective systemic nematicide and can eradicate the normal leaf eelworm infestations in a single treatment. This chemical is also *extremely poisonous and should be handled strictly according to the instructions and with great care.* The nematicide is supplied encapsulated in small hard granules of which about five are placed around the stem of the plant and about $\frac{1}{2}$in below the surface of the compost. The pot plant is placed in an isolated position in the greenhouse and watered normally. During the next six to eight weeks the pot is not touched by hand unless protected by rubber gloves. At the end of the season it is safer to burn the growing medium and destroy the pot. It cannot be stressed enough that this is a most hazardous treatment and, if it is to be used at all, then it should be reserved only for the odd plant which is of real value. It should not even be considered as a general treatment if the infestation is massive.

Temik is, in Great Britain, classified as a Part II

Substance under the Health and Safety (Agricultural) (Poisonous Substances) Regulations and it is essential that full protective clothing, i.e. rubber gauntlet gloves, a full face shield and overall is used at all times when this material is being handled. The sale and use of Temik is restricted to the professional grower and it would be entirely irresponsible for the amateur to handle this extremely toxic chemical.

Stem Rot   Diseases

The probable causative agent is *Botrytis cinerea* and it is all too common a disease to which tuberous begonias are prone, probably because of their soft, fleshy stems. The normal appearance of stem rot is a wet brown patch which spreads quickly throughout the stem. If corrective measures are not taken, then not only will the whole stem collapse, but there is every chance that the rot will ultimately spread to the tuber. The precise cause of an attack is unknown, and indeed there may be many contributory factors to this disease. Certainly overfeeding, especially with high nitrogen fertilisers, causes a softening of the plant tissue so that any infection will spread rapidly. Poor movement of air around the plants will provide an ideal environment for botrytis to flourish so that adequate space and ventilation must be given. Dead and decaying vegetable matter must be cleared away from all parts of the plants. Careless removal of cuttings can damage tissue and unsterilised cutting knives can introduce the botrytis — wounds should always be made cleanly and dusted with green sulphur or a fungicide. Lack of care with the watering can is also a major cause of damage to begonia stems; a short piece of rubber tubing slipped over the spout will reduce the possibility of damage.

Once stem rot has been diagnosed, the severity of the treatment will parallel the severity of the attack. If the patch of rot is limited in area then it should be cut out with a sharp knife which has been sterilised by dipping in methylated spirit. At this point one cannot stress too much the need to remove all the rot, cutting back to absolutely clean tissue. The wet surface of the wound is dried quickly and powdered with a mixture of green sulphur and orthocide. The plant should be inspected regularly at two day intervals to ensure that callousing occurs and the rot has been eliminated. For the next few weeks, the amount of water given to the plant should be reduced and all feeding stopped.

119

If the rot is much more severe, having perhaps completely infected the circumference of the stem, it may be necessary to cut away the whole stem at a point some ³₄in below the infection. This drastic treatment may indeed be the only way of saving the tuber even though it amounts to 'early harvesting'.

Stem rot is more usually associated with the latter part of the season when the night drop in temperature increases the humidity considerably.

Powdery Mildew

It is highly likely that many greenhouses already contain the dormant spores of many mildews and, as long as the environmental conditions remain unfavourable, a mildew attack does not take place. Though one cannot say with certainty what the precise conditions are that enable the spores to develop, it does appear that the combination of low temperature and high humidity make it more likely. Good air circulation will reduce the incidence of an attack. The first sign of mildew is the appearance of a white powdery mark, like cigarette ash, on the leaf surface. The spots rapidly increase in size and number until the whole leaf is affected. Under these circumstances, the mildew will almost certainly have spread to the flowers and buds. Treatment must be carried out quickly if the rapid spread to other plants is to be avoided. In the last decade, a mildew with larger spores has appeared in Britain (*Microsphaera begonia*) and this is resistant to the systemic fungicide Benomyl. A most effective non-systemic fungicide is Dinocap which can be applied by spray or swab to the infected leaves. When plants are in flower then it is better to use Dinocap smoke cones. An alternative fungicide to try is one based on Triforine. Untreated, severe mildew infections will considerably reduce plant vigour. A few begonias do appear to be very susceptible to attacks of mildew, e.g. a number of the B. Rex cultivars, *B. masoniana*, *B. cinnabarina* and, in the tuberhybrida group, the yellow, white and yellow ground picotees. On the other hand, many of the red cultivars are very resistant to mildew.

Bacterial Leaf Spot

At the time of writing, this disease is, fortunately, not often exprienced in Britain though there are signs that its incidence is on the increase. The disease does appear to be more common on Rieger begonias, on the semps, and on the tuberous types. Symptoms of the disease are the appearance of pale green or yellow rings and blotches on the leaves. It is questionable whether a plant, once infected with the bacterium Xanthomonas can be recovered, but if the variety has some special intrinsic value, then an attempt can be made to save it. Any plants which are infected are best removed to a place of quarantine; the remaining plants should be spaced so that they do not touch each other and the greenhouse should be well ventilated to reduce atmospheric humidity. All plants should now be sprayed with a copper fungicide or Bordeaux mixture. This should be repeated over a number of weeks. The plants which are already suffering from the disease should have all the infected parts removed using a sharp knife which is sterilised before and after surgery. The parts removed must be burned. A badly affected plant will not survive, and must be burnt along with the root ball and the pot should also be destroyed. No propagations should be taken from infected plants. Bacterial leaf spot is a very contagious disease and every effort must be made to isolate suspected plants as quickly as possible. The treatment is so severe that it would be best to seek professional advice before embarking on it.

Virus Diseases
As far as can be ascertained tuberous begonias are not known to suffer from any recognisable virus disease. One feature of plants which are known to be infected by virus is that the symptom of the disease reappears year by year, e.g. the colour break in orchids. There are a number of tuberous begonias which do develop leaf markings and these are repeated from year to year. One particular plant will produce mottled leaves which are produced identically each year while other plants of the same cultivar remain free of this defect. As far as one can see, however, the blooms do not appear to be affected.

Anyone who has grown plants (of all types) for any length of time has had the experience of misshapen leaves, yellowing foliage, deformed blooms, brown patches on leaves etc. Usually these problems are fairly transient, disappearing as growth continues or completely absent the following year. Frequently the cause of these problems is unknown, but is probably due to some cultural deficiency. We must await the results of much more investigation into this aspect of begonia cultivation. One or two disorders may, however, be recognised and corrected.

Cultural Disorders

Foliar Petal (Phyllody)
Some tuberous double cultivars, especially those with white, yellow or picotee flowers often produce petals, the edges of

which are green in colour and leaf-like. This phenomenon is restricted to the early flowers and, while it completely spoils the appearance of the flowers, subsequent blooms will usually develop quite normally. The only treatment here is to remove the abnormal buds as soon as the deformity is noticed.

Oedema

Occasionally the underside of the leaves may be marked with small brown areas not unlike the damage caused by an attack of thrip. On examining the marks carefully it may be seen that the surface of the leaf appears pitted and each mark has a shiny, scab-like crust — hence the disorder is sometimes called 'corky scab'. This may be due to the disorder known as Oedema. Plants grown in a moist, closed atmosphere take up considerable quantities of water which they must transpire through their leaves. If the atmospheric humidity is too high, particularly at night, transpiration will be reduced; this can result in the leaf cells bursting followed by a surface rotting of the affected areas. Leaves which still have green areas should be left on the plant to aid transpiration — the ventilation should be increased and all watering should cease after mid afternoon.

Symptoms identical to those of Oedema can also be caused by the use of paraffin heaters at the beginning of the season.

Sun Scorch

Many begonias have soft foliage which scorches easily even under relatively weak sunlight. Light brown patches appear on the leaves and inspection frequently reveals that the scorching has penetrated the whole depth of the leaf. Extensive scorching will retard the plant for weeks. Greenhouse shading is vital and has been discussed on page 36.

Yellow Leaf

The yellowing of foliage from autumn onwards is a natural process and an indication that the plant is preparing for dormancy. During the main part of the growing season, however, yellowing of the lower leaves can be caused by overwatering, cold draughts, low light levels due to overcrowding of plants or a nitrogen deficiency. An application of a high nitrogen fertiliser will correct the problem if it derives from a deficiency.

Bud Drop

This is a common problem which many growers of tuberous

double begonias have experienced. While it may be said that the tendency to shed buds and flowers is occasionally hereditary, it is rarely found in cultivars and more commonly in the mass-produced tubers grown for garden display. The most common reason for bud drop relates to the atmosphere in which the plant is being grown. Hot, arid conditions are completely unsuitable for begonias and will lead to bud and flower drop even with the best cultivars. Overwatering and rapid changes in temperature from day to evening, especially when this is coupled with shutting off ventilation will also heighten the problem. Tuberous double begonias do not make good house plants, but bud drop can be minimised by trying to maintain a fairly uniform temperature of 60°F (16°C) with an atmospheric humidity of about 70 per cent. If one wishes to try and grow tuberous begonias in the house then extra local humidity can be supplied by standing the pots on trays of damp gravel.

Societies and Suppliers

Begonia Societies in Britain and N. America

England and Wales: The National Begonia Society,
Secretary: Dr E. Catterall,
               3 Gladstone Rd.,
               Dorridge,
               Solihull, W. Midlands,
               B93 8BX.

The National Begonia Society has seven areas, each with its own Area Representative:

North West Area Representative:

K. Mitchell,
11 Douglas Ave.,
Stalmine, Blackpool, FY6 0NB.

North East Representative:

R. Curry,
32 Elm Drive, Marton,
Middlesborough,
Cleveland, TS7 5AM.

South East Representative:

A. D. Potty,
36 Norton Ave., Tolworth,
Surrey.

South Coast Representative:

B. Simmons,
136 Chatsworth Ave.,
Cosham, Portsmouth,
Hants. PO6 2UJ.

Yorkshire and Humberside Representative:

J. Rhodes,
7 Tew St., Denby Dale Rd.,
Wakefield.

East Midlands Representative:

S. Greenwood,
41 Alexander Rd.,
Farnsfield, Newark, Notts.
NG22 8LM.

In Scotland: The Scottish Begonia Society,
Secretary: Mrs. I. Hendry,
Clydebridge Lodge,
Greenacre Estate,
Motherwell.

In the USA: The American Begonia Society,
Membership Secretary: Elisabeth Sayers,
369 Ridge Vista Ave.,
San Jose, CA 95127

In Canada: British Columbia Fuchsia and Begonia Society,
Secretary: Mrs. E. I. Hood,
2175 West 16th. Ave.,
Vancouver, B.C. 36K 3B1.
Canada.

Begonia Suppliers in Great Britain

Large-Flowered Double Tuberous and Cascades:

Messrs Blackmore and Langdon,
Stanton Nurseries,
Pensford, Bristol, England.

R. White and Son,
Park Mains Nursery,
Inchinnan, Renfrewshire, Scotland.

Rieger Begonias:

Thomas Rochford and Sons Ltd.,
Turnford Hall Nurseries,
Broxbourne, Herts. EN10 6BH.

Nielsen Plants Ltd.,
Danecroft Nurseries,
Station Rd.,
Hellingley, Sussex BN27 4EU.

Non-Tuberous Begonias:

B. Wall,
4 Selbourne Close, New Haw,
Weybridge, Surrey.

Bedding Begonias of the Fimbriata, Marmorata, Multiflora, Non-Stop, Bertinii etc. Types:

Spalding Bulb Co. Ltd.,
Spalding, Lincs. PE11 1NA.

J. Parker Dutch Bulbs Co.,
452 Chester Rd., Old Trafford, Manchester M16 9HL.

Multiflora Begonias, Semperflorens etc.:

Samuel Dobie and Son Ltd.,
Upper Dee Mills,
Llangollen,
Cllwyd, LL20 8SD.

Suttons Ltd.,
Hele Rd.,
Torquay, Devon TQ2 7QJ.

Begonia Suppliers in the USA

Kartuz Greenhouses Inc.,
1408 Sunset Drive,
Vista, CA 92083.

Logee's Greenhouses,
Dept. B,
55 North St.,
Danielson,
CT 06239.

Antonelli Bros.,
2545 Capitola Rd.,
Santa Cruz,
CA 95060.

Bibliography

Bedson, Frederick, *Successful Begonia Culture*, (W. H. & L. Collingridge, 1954)

Fogg, H. G. Witham, *Begonias, Gloxinias, and African Violets*, (John Gifford, 1967)

Genders, Roy, *Begonias*, (John Gifford, 1958)

Haegeman, J., *Tuberous Begonias*, (J. Cramer, 1979)

Langdon, Brian, *The Tuberous Begonia*, (Cassell, 1969)

Thompson, Mildred L. and Edward J., *Begonias. The Complete Reference Guide*, (Times Books, 1981)

Index

Index

Index